Cold War Criticism
and the Politics
of Skepticism

Cold War Criticism and the Politics of Skepticism

TOBIN SIEBERS

New York   Oxford
OXFORD UNIVERSITY PRESS
1993

Oxford University Press

Oxford New York Toronto
Delhi Bombay Calcutta Madras Karachi
Kuala Lumpur Singapore Hong Kong Tokyo
Nairobi Dar es Salaam Cape Town
Melbourne Auckland Madrid

and associated companies in
Berlin Ibadan

Copyright © 1993 by Oxford University Press, Inc.

Published by Oxford University Press, Inc.,
200 Madison Avenue, New York, New York 10016

Oxford is a registered trademark of Oxford University Press

Library of Congress Cataloging-in-Publication Data
Siebers, Tobin. 1953–
Cold War criticism and the politics of skepticism / Tobin Siebers.
p. cm. — (Odéon)
Includes index.
ISBN 0–19–507964–7. — ISBN 0–19–507965–5 (pbk.)
1. Criticism—Political aspects. 2. Cold War in literature.
3. Politics and literature. 4. Critical theory. 5. Skepticism.
I. Title.
PN98.P64S54 1993
801'.95'09045—dc20 92–23376

9 8 7 6 5 4 3 2 1

Printed in the United States of America
on acid-free paper

For Jill, Claire, and Pierce

Preface

This book engages the politics of the skeptical criticism of the cold war era on two levels. On the one hand, I propose a political analysis that traces critical theory's relation to particular political events and attitudes in the world, most often to events of the cold war era.* My claim is that modern criticism is a cold war criticism, and I attempt to argue the case by juxtaposing the positions taken by postwar critics and the prevailing political attitudes of their times. Current events and popular attitudes shape the spirit of cold war criticism in a powerful way. In a sense, it would be absurd to believe otherwise, despite the many attempts on the part of critics to convince us that they exist beyond the clash of the world.

On the other hand, I analyze cold war criticism in terms of its dominant political language, making clear how its metaphors create ideals of community, polity, and the political process. It is a major issue of this book, however, whether language should be made the unique basis of politics. Part of my criticism of cold war theory will be to point out that its use of the term "political" is too abstract and

---

*Remarkable changes have occurred in the postwar order of the world during the writing of this book. I have deliberately left benchmarks of these changes in order to record the historical pressures that bore upon my writing. I feel comfortable with this decision because this book is not a work of history but of critical theory.

unworldly. It is questionable whether this type of politics can be said to be political at all. It is, more typically, a refusal of politics disguised as high moral or political argument, but I will be claiming that a politics that takes to the high wire is merely an "act" and makes little practical contribution to the world. I expend energy on this type of analysis only because I want to make obvious the terms of my disagreement with skeptical criticism.

Both types of analysis lead me to the conclusion that the desire to forgo a grounding in the world, rather than providing a radical critique of politics, leaves the skeptical criticism of the cold war period without a political direction. Skepticism drifts toward dogmatism and conservatism as readily as toward disbelief and radicalism. To say that skeptical criticism is directionless is to assert its essentially apolitical nature, to expose its fear of taking political positions, and to explain that the dogma espoused by skeptical critics, where "everything is political," is primarily a means of fleeing from politics. Politics demands that we risk taking a position, that we stand somewhere, that we decide, and that we accept as part of the political process the possibility that our positions, stances, and decisions may go horribly wrong, nowhere, or miraculously right. This is the only form of arbitrariness, a favorite term of skeptical criticism, worth talking about and with which it is important to live. The possibility of arbitrariness and risk in the political process is the only good rationale for binding ourselves to skepticism.

By enlarging the description of skeptical criticism, of its resistances to dogmatism, and of the ways in which these resistances turn toward dogmatism and reactionary politics, I am seeking, polemically, to make a contribution to our age of skepticism. I say "polemically" because my method is to test skeptical positions repeatedly before turning to alternative suggestions about how criticism might go about the business of finding a home in the world. None of these alternatives, however, is free of the skeptical temperament since I do not believe that a position purified of skepticism exists. In fact, the desire for logical hygiene is today more characteristic of skepticism than of any other attitude. Each chapter covers a single aspect of skepticism and attacks from a different direction, but skepticism remains intact at the end of this book, if only in the obstinate doubts that I myself feel about the skeptical project of the cold war years.

In chapter 1 I offer an introductory sketch of skepticism, its political metaphors, and the psychology of the skeptical critic. Here my main objective is to provide a description of the soft psychology found at the heart of skepticism. Skeptical hermeneutics, I argue, implies a basic psychology that skeptics design for themselves in order to enforce an unwarranted claim to political, ethical, and intellectual power. The remaining chapters analyze various ethical and political applications of this position, especially issues related to World War II and the cold war. I take up debates concerning the conflict of interpretations, symbolic action, cultural literacy and multiculturalism, the Holocaust, the politics of interpretation, and the collaborationist writings of Paul de Man and Martin Heidegger in order to show that the radicalism of skeptical critics may produce effects contrary to their political agendas. In chapter 2 I illustrate the concept of cold war criticism by linking the rhetoric of four postwar critics—W. K. Wimsatt and Monroe Beardsley, Geoffrey Hartman, and Stephen Greenblatt—to the cold war period as it evolved from Churchill's "Iron Curtain" speech to the close of the Reagan presidency and the fall of the Berlin Wall. In chapter 3 I examine recent debates about comparative literature and multiculturalism in order to draw some distinctions between ethics and politics that are necessary to describe the politics of skeptical criticism and its alternatives. In chapter 4 I provide a more detailed picture of the politics of the skeptical critic in the person of Paul de Man. I begin by arguing that de Man's linguistic theories attempt to exhaust the rhetoric of the self but end by affirming it through an act of mourning. I continue this reading in the political context established by the discovery of de Man's wartime journalism and Nazi connections in order to chart how mourning turns political. Here my purpose is threefold: to place de Man in the political environment of World War II; to read him from a psychoanalytic point of view (that is, in terms of the orthodoxy most difficult for deconstruction to disavow); and to expose how his theories purchase political power and charisma for the character of the critic. In chapter 5, on Paul de Man and Jane Tompkins, I ask how our theories of interpretation affect our practical relationship to the classroom, and provide another illustration of the idea that modern theory owes an enormous debt to the cold war. I also stress the notion that interpretation is a form of political storytelling that emphasizes dialogue and knowledge of the world. In chapter 6 I continue this political emphasis by summarizing Hannah Arendt's powerful view of the politics of judgment and storytelling and by analyzing her ideas about the Holocaust, the languages of destiny, movement, and history, and the virtues of being at home in the world of interpretation. Finally, in chapter 7 I elaborate upon the idea that the "post" in poststructuralism and postmodernism alludes to the postwar world. I also describe some ways in which these schools of criticism seek refuge in the past to escape the present, and conclude by offering a few suggestions about what theory must do if it is to enter the post–cold war era successfully.

It is an irony of this book that it will be least agreeable to those who can best understand it and most acceptable to those who may never read it. My language is, by and large, the discourse of modern critical theory, but I am more interested in criticizing than in supporting this discourse because it isolates critical thought in a world of its own. Among the many ideas that cold war theorists have refused to consider is the notion that literary criticism is out of touch with what in academia we like to call the "real world." Cold war criticism has every interest in remaining blind to this truth as long as it refuses to view itself with the same skeptical regard that it directs toward everything else. My purpose here is to suggest that the interest in turning toward the world is greater than ignoring it, although this action is risky and frightening. My own language, then, springs neither from self-defeating impulses nor from the desire to marginalize myself within my own discipline. It is the consequence of an evolution in my thoughts about literature, criticism, and the world. I offer these polemics in the hope that they might motivate a few people to think about what they do in a different light. As for me, I remain firm in my resolve to develop a form of address whose intelligibility, purpose, and usefulness are oriented toward everyday life. I ask those readers interested in a less polemical evaluation of the relations among ethics, politics, and literature to consider my work in *Morals and Stories* (New York: Columbia University Press, 1992). It is less a battle cry than this effort, but its purpose springs from the same motivations that prompted this book.

Ann Arbor, Mich.   T.S.
July 1992

Acknowledgments

I would like to express my gratitude to the John Simon Guggenheim Memorial Foundation for the fellowship that made possible the writing of various parts of this book. Sandor Goodhart, Andrew McKenna, and Peter Walker invited me to speak at the Modern Language Association, the Midwest Modern Language Asssociation, and the University of Minnesota at Duluth, respectively, giving me the opportunity to formulate some of the positions expressed here. I also benefited from comments by Julie Ellison and appreciate the help of Josué Harari, who found the book within the book. Finally, special thanks go to Linda Gregerson and Steven Mullaney, at whose table the idea for this book was born.

I am grateful to the editors of *Common Knowledge, The New Orleans Review, The Southern Humanities Review,* and the University of Nebraska Press for permissions to reprint various materials, all of which have been revised.

Contents

Cold War Criticism
and the Politics
of Skepticism

Only the pauper sings before the highwayman.

Juvenal

1

Introduction:
The Politics of Skepticism

Critical theorists today share an attitude that is not easily shared with others. They share skepticism. Skeptics question not only the nature of specific truths but the interests that guide human action. They attempt to think beyond the limits of their own self-interests, whatever the specific matter at issue. In ethics, skeptical thinkers question the possibility of ethical behavior as such, denouncing altruism as disguised egotism. In politics, they assert their belief that power contaminates social organization and that the lust for power masquerades as the desire for justice. In aesthetics, they claim that beauty is hardly a disinterested concept but another word for ideology.

What does it mean to share such attitudes with other people? What does it mean to constitute a community on the basis of something like skepticism? In sum, what is the politics of skepticism? "Skepticism," an old definition says, "is a sect of people who speak otherwise than they think!" We may rewrite this definition in terms of the project of philosophical skepticism that has been joined to critical theory to define skeptics as those people who think otherwise than they think. For skepticism now describes more than anything else the project of opposing thought to itself.[1]

---

[1] The philosopher on the current scene most illuminating about skepticism is Stanley Cavell. I confess that I am unclear about how my formulations relate to his, since I am

The smallest dose of skepticism goes a long way. Its deadly potency kills with ease forests of symbols. But one cannot be skeptical of anything today and still retain one's credentials in the eyes of other skeptics. Can one claim the title of skeptic and doubt the skeptical truths found on the current scene? Can one legitimately question, for example, the orthodoxies of Freud, Marx, and Nietzsche; whether power masquerades as truth; whether the self, reality, or gender are constructs; whether language is violent; whether radical hermeneutics translate into radical politics; or whether belief (metaphysics) is an obsolete category, and continue to retain one's skeptical papers?

Kant, of course, opened the age of criticism when he introduced the idea of the "critical" as the philosophical view that would break down such long-standing oppositions as skepticism and dogmatism. If we are to believe in Kant's project, with which our own ideas of criticism are inextricably linked, we must accept the basic principle that skepticism and dogmatism are sufficiently different that it is philosophically worthwhile to show that they resemble each other. But such acceptance may no longer be possible because modern skepticism regulates itself according to obvious dogmatisms, while the strongest modern dogmatists often embrace positions that have belonged historically to skepticism. Kant threw a bridge across the gulf between skepticism and dogmatism, but little did he know that the armies of skepticism would

---

interested in describing the ethical and political effects of cold war skepticism, but I am encouraged by his descriptions of Descartes's thinking process, in which Descartes's drive to think of himself as "a thing that thinks" makes him consider the proposition that his head might have turned into clay or that he might be a gourd. Cavell does not make the point, to my knowledge, that this phantasm is something of a fulfillment of the desire to become a "thinking thing," but his notion that skepticism attempts to reach in thought those places impossible for thought to reach generally captures the idea. My project here is to locate this confusion between self-defeat and the desire for logical purity in a political and social context in order to expose the paradox by which the politics of skepticism turn apolitical: my thesis is that skeptics attempt to occupy political and ethical positions that mean the end of politics and ethics. On Cartesian skepticism, see Stanley Cavell, "Being Odd, Getting Even (Descartes, Emerson, Poe)," in his *In Quest of the Ordinary* (Chicago: University of Chicago Press, 1988), 105–30, and, on skepticism in general, *The Claim of Reason: Wittgenstein, Skepticism, Morality, and Tragedy* (New York: Oxford University Press, 1979).

march across it to conquer the throne of dogmatism and so set up a kingdom in their enemy's house.

Whence another old saying about skepticism: "Many a skeptical saying is nothing more than a borrowed article, picked up and retailed by those who say it because it seems clever." That there may be a retail market for skepticism exposes a truth: skepticism has achieved an institutional status in which rules apply to its practice. An economy depends upon it, and skeptics depend upon this economy for their livelihood. There are now limits to thinking otherwise if one wishes to remain a skeptic.

It is not clear that one can, in this critical age, avoid being a skeptic. We are, it seems, bound to be skeptical. But the project of thinking otherwise need not follow the dogmatic lines of skepticism as we know them. To think otherwise about one's own silent skepticism is another possibility. But what would this mean? Thinking against skepticism would attempt to reveal the dogmatic side of the most skeptical positions and to locate perspectives that skeptics have opposed not because they have thoughtfully rejected them but because these perspectives threaten their own personal skepticism. It would test arguments and points of view inimical to skepticism. It would try to isolate those rules by which a successful skeptical argument in one intellectual domain is allowed too easily to slip over the border into another domain and lay claim to it, without having had to argue its way. It would make sure that skeptics do not play by the rules of dogmatists. Indeed, whether the skeptic should be playing by any rules at all is a burning question for both skeptics and their critics.

To be skeptical about skepticism is either the most reactionary of philosophies or the most radical. But how are we to tell which? In the era of suspicion par excellence, the cold war era, such an attitude is more likely to be called reactionary or conservative. But, first, it is not clear that political labels such as "conservative," "reactionary," "liberal," or "radical" are worth applying directly to philosophical argument. This is one more modern practice worth being skeptical about, and it is not "conservative" to do so. And, second, it is not certain that one may travel back to belief by way of being skeptical about skepticism because the skeptical temperament continues to dominate our age. In others words, I want to establish a difference between thinkers who defend certain so-called traditional ideas against skepticism and those whose enmity to skepticism tends to situate them on the side of traditional ideas for the sole reason that our intellectual maps do not know where else to place them. This latter position takes skeptical argument almost more seriously than the skeptics themselves do and is forced into a skepticism about skepticism because rigorous thought permits no other choice. It defines itself as a critique of skepticism and directs its disillusionment for the most part toward it, whereas the skeptic ends by being disappointed by various institutions and beliefs. The strength of this position is that it acts as a critical watchdog for skepticism, requiring that it take itself seriously, seek out applications for its insights, and not turn into a mere strategy for gaining the moral high ground in argumentation. The weakness of this position is that it may perhaps fall into an unreflective dogmatism, if it lets down its critical guard, because it is less concerned with dogmatism than with skepticism.

Michel Foucault's last work on the history of sexuality may partially illuminate this position, although he is not often given to unreflective dogmatism. It has been hard for a skeptical audience to accept this work as one more skeptical turn in a career marked by many such turns. Foucault was, of course, the thinker who won popularity (perhaps with Louis Althusser) for the idea that the "human," as an explanatory concept, must be replaced by "language." Then, unexpectedly, he turned in his last writings (*The Use of Pleasure* and *The Care of the Self*) to a description of the ethico-poetic self, where both beauty and truth are achieved through a sustained process of ascesis or self-mastery.[2] Longtime acquaintances as well as critics who had supported Foucault suddenly found themselves in violent disagreement with him.[3] His idea of an ascetic homosexuality was especially annoy-

[2] References are to Michel Foucault, *The Use of Pleasure,* trans. Robert Hurley (New York: Pantheon, 1985).

[3] The most obvious example is Leo Bersani's "Pedagogy and Pederasty," *Raritan* 5, no. 1 (1985): 14–21. Bersani calls the transgressive analysis in the first volume of *The History of Sexuality* "brilliant" but has "harsh remarks" for the second and third volumes. He

ing to a community of theorists who had relied on him for a description of transgressive and jubilant desire; and they accused him of throwing in with the repressive and conservative institutions that he had always opposed. But Foucault himself portrayed the turn in his thought as an exercise in the activity of thought, a "philosophical exercise" in which the objective "was to learn to what extent the effort to think one's own history can free thought from what it silently thinks, and so enable it to think differently" (9). To be skeptical of Foucault, the thinker of the "death of man," was to become Foucault, the thinker of the hermeneutics of the self.[4]

The project of doubting skepticism did not necessarily produce Foucault's new hermeneutics, but his desire to think differently did produce an argument that has been interpreted by his critics to contradict his previous skeptical positions. It is one of life's little ironies that the modern thinker most associated with the thinking of "otherness" was attacked by longtime supporters of alterity because he had begun to think too differently from other people; and that these critics argued their positions by accusing Foucault of contradicting himself, as if, suddenly, "contradiction" had become a curse word instead of a compliment in their lingo. I am reminded of two somewhat different but related stories that expose the absurdities that such earnest skepticism is sometimes heir to. Academic folklore has it that the organizers of the legendary conference on schizo-analysis in New York City—featuring Foucault, Deleuze and Guattari, and others—decided to invite various marginals and indigents to the proceedings, but when the honored guests were forced to listen to the theoretical discourse on otherness, they revolted, stormed the podium, and drove the speakers from the auditorium. Another piece of academic folklore relates how some

---

accuses Foucault of glamorizing the renunciation of sex for the sake of power, of succumbing to the temptation to view history and philosophy as free, nonconditioned exercises of the mind rather than as particular versions of the mind's conformity to its culture, and of desexualizing the very act of writing to seek austerity.

[4]Edward Said in his homage to Foucault, "Michel Foucault, 1927–1984," *Raritan* 4, no. 2 (1984): 1–11, emphasizes this skepticism as well as the irony that the philosopher of the "death of man" was himself "the very example of what a truly remarkable, unmistakably eccentric and individual thing a human life really is" (11).

avant-garde Parisian theorists received it as a deliciously transgressive maneuver when René Girard, in *Things Hidden Since the Foundation of the World*, defended the Immaculate Conception of Mary and confessed his belief in the divinity of Christ. Such are the unexpected opportunities for amusement in the world of intellectual fashion.

Sudden contrasts in academic positions do not always have such comic results, especially when they involve ethical and political matters. Often the contradiction between what critics are supposed to believe and what they are actually arguing is jarring, the result of either bad thought, bad faith, or bad politics. Paul de Man, for example, is generally considered one of our most radical literary theorists, and yet his arguments clash oddly with the politics of his times. In 1972 and 1973, when he was writing the bulk of *Allegories of Reading* (sections of which appeared in such leading journals as *Critical Inquiry, Diacritics, and Glyph*), Richard Nixon was reelected and then forced to resign as president, the student movement was winning the protest against the Vietnam War, the university had raised the banner of relevance in the classroom, the women's movement had emerged, and the satirical television program "All in the Family" was at the zenith of its popularity. Nevertheless, de Man opens his book by praising formalism and attacking "relevance," and fortifies his case with a rhetorical analysis of "All in the Family," in which a remark by Archie Bunker helps him to explicate deconstructive theory. De Man focuses on an argument between Archie and Edith Bunker over the meaning of the phrase, "What's the difference?," and claims that Archie's frustration with it exposes the instability of rhetorical questions in particular and of language in general. Surprisingly, the radical theorist makes his case by identifying deconstruction with the notoriously right-winged, sexist, and bigoted Archie and ends his argument by calling Jacques Derrida and Nietzsche "archie de-Bunkers" (9).[5]

---

[5] References are to Paul de Man's *Allegories of Reading* (New Haven, Conn.: Yale University Press, 1979). De Man obviously means to write "arche de-Bunkers" but slips Derrida and Nietzsche into Archie's shoes. These comments were originally published as "Semiology and Rhetoric," *Diacritics* 3, no. 3 (1973): 27–33, during the height of the popularity of "All in the Family." Two superb readings of this essay make good cases for the similarity between de Man's and Archie Bunker's positions. See Stanley Cavell, "The Politics of Interpretation (Politics as Opposed to What?)," in his *Themes Out of School*

If being a radical theorist sometimes leads to reactionary analogies, we might well consider becoming more lenient toward those who embrace conservative criticism just in case they are preparing to become politically liberal. But, of course, this is not the point. The point is that our usual political terminology may change when we bring it into the theater of literary criticism, but it is not necessarily wise to accept these new meanings because political labels are best understood in political contexts. From what we know of de Man's political history, he was conservative at best, and just because his theories of literature upset the narrowly defined status quo in academia does not mean that he should be called "radical." Moreover, it is likely that de Man's formalism, although intimidating to some, ensured that his ideas would have little political application, and consequently his theories helped in many ways to insulate the study of literature from radical trends at precisely the moment in history when they were most threatening. In this light, de Man's claim that "reading . . . has to go against the grain of what one would want to happen in the name of what has to happen" sounds like a program for resisting the liberal reforms of his era and for affirming the dire necessities voiced by the conservative right; and his celebrated "rigor" and "authority" begin to seem schoolmarmish.[6]

By contrast, Foucault, even at his most "conservative" moment, continued to possess a transgressive and polemical spirit because his ideas were both controversial and had an immediate claim on everyday experience and conduct. His subjects were, after all, the hospital, the prison, and modern mores. Edward Said is another theorist who, like Foucault, wears his politics on his sleeve, and whether one agrees with him is less important than the possibilities that he has brought to literary criticism for involvement in the world outside the academy. On the other hand, the Marxist critic Fredric Jameson, while claiming a radical politics, offers no such "radicalness" in his interpretation of

---

(San Francisco: North Point Press, 1984), and Ellen Rooney, *Seductive Reasoning: Pluralism as the Problematic of Contemporary Literary Theory* (Ithaca, N.Y.: Cornell University Press, 1989), 188–92.

[6] See the foreword to Carol Jacobs, *The Dissimulating Harmony* (Baltimore: Johns Hopkins University Press, 1978), xi.

literature. *The Political Unconscious,* arguably the most influential
Marxist essay on the current scene, never quite makes the leap from
theory to practice. It opens with a "slogan" and "moral," "Always
historicize!," which Jameson calls "the one absolute and we may even
say 'transhistorical' imperative of all dialectical thought" (9). But as a
slogan it apparently has little purchase since Jameson shows no loyalty
to it: he prefers to use early structuralist theory, such as the semiotic
rectangle of A. J. Greimas, to interpret texts rather than to delve into
their history. And as a moral it is dubious because Jameson himself
argues against the tendency to engage in ethical criticism and claims
that ethics is a rhetoric that appropriates its power by ignoring historical contingencies.[7] The proof of this dubious but widely held idea
about ethics would apparently be that Jameson's singular moral about
history, "Always historicize!," is the one absolute and transhistorical
imperative.[8]

At the other end of the political spectrum stands the criticism of
Wayne Booth. Booth is certainly not opposed to ethical criticism, having recently completed a huge tome on the ethics of fiction entitled *The
Company We Keep.*[9] The book is enormously generous and so lacking
in mean-spiritedness that I feel almost ashamed to disagree with it. But,
in some ways, Booth has the same problem as Jameson. Both want to
see literature as a socially symbolic act, Booth for ethics and Jameson
for politics, but social relations remain largely "symbolic" for them in
the final analysis because they have difficulty crossing from the do-

[7] General references are to Fredric Jameson, *The Political Unconscious: Narrative as a
Socially Symbolic Act* (Ithaca, N.Y.: Cornell University Press, 1981). On ethics Jameson
writes: "In its narrowest sense, ethical thought projects as permanent features of human
'experience,' and thus as a kind of 'wisdom' about personal life and interpersonal
relations, what are in reality the historical and institutional specifics of a determinate
type of group solidarity or class cohesion" (59). This is perhaps the place to say that I
approve of Jameson's sense, if I read him correctly, that the attack on "humanism" by
Derridean and Althusserian groups turns "idealistic" itself when it reads this category as
a "transhistorical" error and not in terms of the grounds of the most everyday attitudes
and presuppositions (59n.36).

[8] See Geoffrey Galt Harpham's analysis of this phrase in "Language, History, Ethics,"
Raritan 7, no. 1 (1987): 128–46, esp. 146.

[9] References are to Wayne C. Booth, *The Company We Keep: An Ethics of Fiction*
(Berkeley and Los Angeles: University of California Press, 1988).

mains of formalism and aesthetics into the social world. In Booth's case the problem occurs when he must reject a work or author as ethically undesirable. Booth considers such rejection only as a last resort. He is adamant that we "open ourselves to 'others' that look initially dangerous or worthless" (488). Booth's argument is attractive precisely because he is so careful in his polemics against authors. He shows respect for writers and their works in an age when the dominant critical attitude toward them is doubt, if not contempt. But an ethics of fiction must sooner or later decide what it can and cannot embrace, if it is not to be a shadow ethics, and here Booth falters because his rejections are actually aesthetically, not ethically motivated. He cannot support the company of Peter Benchley's *Jaws*, *Penthouse* magazine, and Rabelais, although he hesitates more than once before rejecting the last. All three treat women in despicable ways, but I think that Booth would be hard put to justify his rejection on these grounds, since the texts are certainly not among the worst offenders in this regard. The real key is that the first two have no status in belles lettres, and Rabelais writes in a way that is hard to handle according to modern aesthetic standards. It is as if any one of them could have been saved for ethical criticism, if only they were written better. Jane Austen, for example, also receives sharp criticism on feminist grounds, but Booth keeps her within his ethical fold because *Emma* may be recuperated as "ironic," in short, by reference to one of the most important categories of modern aesthetics.[10]

These cases should make clear that the ethics and politics of criticism do not necessarily conform to the everyday meanings of the terms and that the attempt to use ethical and political labels to define critical agendas may turn controversial when we traverse different areas of description. One problem is that we tend to interpret ethical and political descriptions of the critical act as if they were actually positions in

[10] Booth's position here collapses into that of J. Hillis Miller in *The Ethics of Reading* (New York: Columbia University Press, 1987). Miller argues that an ethics of reading manifests itself by affirming the undecidable character of language. Similar to the New Critics' view of "irony" and "paradox," Miller's position celebrates ambiguity as the essential quality of poetic language, here as its ethical rather than aesthetic quality. Booth's redemption of Austen for ethical criticism also follows this aesthetic imperative.

the world, when their function most often is to eschew the political plane of existence in order to win a charismatic and worldless subjectivity for the critic. This preoccupation with the character of the critic does not leave ethics and politics behind—indeed, a strong ethical and political tint colors the way that skeptics describe their critical powers, and even the most unworldly of skepticisms touches down in the political world—but it may, perhaps, be considered with greater justice in terms of a certain "soft psychology." The beliefs against which skeptical critics define themselves are viewed largely as "constructions" that bring comfort to those incapable of facing the truth of radical doubt. Constructions of belief make meaning possible, according to skeptics, but they also serve a psychological function defined as the need of most people (except skeptics) to conceal from themselves the terrible fact that existence either has no meaning or relies on oppressive relations of power. These constructions range from religious belief proper to a number of equally obvious categories, including reality, the self, the West, gender, history, and sexuality. Belief as a category has become psychologically and epistemologically suspect, and skeptical theorists inevitably try to describe ways of knowing that are more aware of the various forms of false consciousness into which human beings fall. But it is impossible in many instances to see these attempts as anything other than a psychological and moral drama that ends in paradox because people find it difficult to believe in something when belief is the target of their skepticism. Skeptics define their virtue as critics in direct proportion to their ability to purify their thinking of "beliefs," and this despite the fact that a founding tenet of modern skepticism holds that there exists no position independent of the constructions of belief. The current scene therefore abounds with descriptions of the minimal conditions of belief, the minimal aspect being a direct result of the feverish effort on the part of skeptics to reduce belief to its lowest power.

I will content myself here with giving a brief analysis of how skepticism affects a few recent descriptions of reality, axiology, and subjectivity, my immediate purpose being to uncover the psychological drama in trying to think without the constructions of belief and my ultimate purpose being to demonstrate the ways in which this drama encounters ethical and political difficulties. My method, then, is not merely to leap from one pole of a binary opposition to the other in order to prove that skeptics rely on the dogmas that they critique, although this will be part of my argument. Nor am I interested solely in the self-refutation of various arguments. All logical assertion, if read in a certain way, is self-refuting. This is the central insight of deconstruction. But this insight has no general consequences for interpretation, although it has many particular ones. The need, then, is to form an interpretation at the level of particular consequences and to make visible the conflicts of interpretation. This type of interpretation goes in this book by the name of "politics." More specifically, my objective here is to describe the critical cross fire between radical positions in literary criticism and reactionary ones in ethics and politics, and sometimes vice versa.

It may be worth noting at the outset how parasitic is skeptical criticism's general relationship to belief. Those works seminal to structural analysis—Vladimir Propp on the folktale and Tzvetan Todorov on the fantastic, for example—take as their objects of study the literature of belief. Deconstruction in a certain sense can be said to be interested only in the trappings of metaphysics. Jonathan Culler, to cite a recent example, has gone so far as to redefine an entire field of literary study, comparative literature, in opposition to religious belief.[11] Culler writes of comparative literature that "its most precise characteristic is to be what others are not," thereby embracing the skeptical project of thinking otherwise with a vengeance (30). What comparative literature is definitely not, if we follow Culler's scary formulation, is a mode of thinking that succumbs to the "dangerous American notion that toleration requires one not to mock, criticize, or even discuss other people's religious beliefs" (31). Rather, comparative literature should follow its "Enlightenment heritage," embrace the proud tradition of the critique of religion, and take up the slogan, "Down with the priests!" (30, 32). Cold war criticism, it appears, lives in proximity to what it most

[11]Jonathan Culler, "Comparative Literature and the Pieties," *Profession 86* (1986):30–32. On the one hand, Culler calls for an enlightened anticlericism that unflinchingly attacks the pieties of religion. On the other hand, he is, on the current theoretical scene, one of the major proponents of indeterminacy as an interpretive principle. See Jonathan Culler, *Flaubert: The Uses of Uncertainty* (Ithaca, N.Y.: Cornell University Press, 1974).

detests. It has embarked on a reverse crusade, where glory is won not by freeing the Holy Land but by destroying it, and if people like Culler have any say in the matter, this situation will not soon be improving.

The representation of reality on the current scene, to take my first category, finds its minimal description in the work of the historian Hayden White.[12] White's "Value of Narrativity in the Representation of Reality" takes as its challenge the question: "What would a nonnarrative representation of historical reality look like?" (4).[13] For an answer White turns to the "annals" model of history, in which lists of dates accompanied and unaccompanied by events are typical (6–7). These events do not have any implicit connection to one another, and their recorders have made no attempt to create a narrative that would justify their coexistence in the same documents. Rather, the annals present what appears to be a list of stark and random happenings:

711.

712.   Flood everywhere.

713.

714.   Pippin, mayor of the palace, died.

[12] Also contributing to the minimal description of reality on the current scene is Louis O. Mink, "Narrative Form as a Cognitive Instrument," in *Historical Understanding,* ed. Brian Fay, Eugene O. Golub, and Richard T. Vann (Ithaca, N.Y.: Cornell University Press, 1987), 182–203. Mink notices that we may possess a scientific knowledge of how a watch works, but another form of knowledge exists in the story of the watch's "career," that is, how it has been produced, shipped, stored, displayed, purchased, used, lost, and so forth. Narrative knowledge escapes theoretical understanding, in Mink's view, because to envision a history of the watch "requires the attribution of indefinitely many descriptions of it as they are successively relevant or irrelevant to the sequences that intersect its career" (185). Mink nevertheless find this narrative understanding significant and links it to the cognitive value of literature. He claims, for example, that *Ulysses* may tell us more about life in Dublin than any historical account, even though few of its events really take place. I mention this line of argument because Mink's affirmation of the cognitive value of literature limits his skepticism. It also provides a view of interpretation that frees it sufficiently from skepticism that it might go about the business of finding a home in the world. While Mink does not put this view of interpretation to political use, it is, in my eyes, at the heart of politics.

[13] References are to Hayden White, "The Value of Narrativity in the Representation of Reality," *The Content of Form* (Baltimore: Johns Hopkins University Press, 1987), 1–25. For a powerful critique compatible with my remarks, see David Carr, *Time, Narrative, and History* (Bloomington: Indiana University Press, 1986), 1–17.

715.   716.   717.
718.   Charles devastated the Saxon with great destruction.
719.

White describes annals writing as a vision of a culture hovering on
the brink of dissolution, "a society of radical scarcity, a world of
human groups threatened by death, devastation, flood, and famine"
(7). Moreover, this vision of destruction is itself incomprehensible. The
entries describe events, White confesses, whose "importance consists
in nothing other than their having been recorded" (7). The annals
provide a view of reality in which constructions such as narrative,
morality, politics, religion, logic, and subjectivity do not exist. The
only constructed order is the sequence of dates. Reality unconstructed
and unstoried has this appearance.

White argues that unlike the reality of the annals, historical reality as
we usually describe it wears "the mask of a meaning" (21). It seeks
closure, explanation, cause and effect, and fullness. Historical reality is
false, White concludes, because it is the product of moral beliefs that
try to give us the comfort of objectivity, seriousness, and realism.
"What I have sought to suggest," he concedes, "is that this value
attached to narrativity in the representation of real events arises out of
a *desire* to have real events display the coherence, integrity, fullness,
and closure of an image of life that is and can only be *imaginary*. . . . Does the world really present itself to perception in the form
of well-made stories, with central subjects, proper beginnings, middles,
and ends, and a coherence that permits us to see 'the end' in every
beginning? Or does it present itself . . . as mere sequence without
beginning or end or as sequences of beginnings that only terminate and
never conclude?" (24; emphases mine).

The answer to these questions according to White is that reality is a
mere sequence of brute facts. Although his view of reality may not be
as comforting as the traditional one, this does not mean that it provides
no comfort. It expresses what has become a standard description of
reality for the age of skepticism, and it displays the influence of our
postwar view of reality, which fears narrative and prefers fragmentation to wholeness; but it is nevertheless as vulnerable to skepticism as

any other standard description. If the real, we may ask, is a random occurrence of sheer happenings, and we narrativize it out of a desire for order, from where does this desire come? Why is human desire so unreal, so unnatural? Here it becomes obvious that White's epistemology has an implicit psychology and that we are forced to accept his description of desire not on the basis of argument but as a consequence of his theory of reality. He provides no demonstration of why we should want to believe that desire is ordered, whereas reality is not. Perhaps his theory of reality is the result of a mobile and shattered desire that manifests itself by redescribing the perfect order of reality as chaos. At this point a classic Lacanian interpretation would begin to talk about the aggressivity of the self, narcissistic disorders, imaginary relations, and phallic mothers. Lacan describes this view of reality as "the especial delusion of the misanthropic *'belle âme,'* throwing back on to the world the disorder of which his being is composed" (20).[14] There is no reason to prefer White's pre-1920 Freudianism, in which desire finds pleasure in stability, to a late Freudian and Lacanian psychology in which desire leaps beyond the pleasure principle into a vertiginous unpleasure.

Notice that I am not arguing that reality is perfectly coherent or incoherent, for I do not know what reality looks like. I am merely applying an alternate, trendy description to make a point not about reality but about the dogmatic side of White's skepticism: his skeptical theory of reality is as much a "story" as the traditional view that he opposes. But why are we more likely to believe his story than the other one? The answer is that White's story is compatible with the standard version of skepticism.

Barbara Herrnstein Smith's forays into axiology have made virtues of the contingency of value and of alternate descriptions. Like White she wishes to dispose of the grand narrative constructions of reality—what she sometimes calls "ur-stories"—in order to reveal the radical contingency of these constructions and of our valuations of them. *The Contingencies of Value* is perhaps the ultimate in thinking otherwise because Smith claims that her interest lies in neither assertion nor

[14] Jacques Lacan, "Aggressivity in Psychoanalysis," in his *Ecrits: A Selection,* trans. Alan Sheridan (New York: Norton, 1977), 8–29.

denial of "assertion-in-itself" or of "truth-in-itself" but in an *alternate description* of what is *otherwise described* as 'assertion,' 'denial,' and 'truth'" (113; Smith's emphases).[15] Alternate descriptions of objects and events are reduced to one story, according to Smith, in order to have an objective, value-free account. But no objective account exists, in Smith's opinion, because all value is contingent.

Entertaining alternate descriptions is nevertheless a value in itself for Smith, despite her claims against the noncontingency of any value, and her project stakes its virtue on its persistent and systematic opposition to objectivist axiology. Her major claim about the objectivist, in stark contrast to her own goals, remains that he (Smith uses the masculine pronoun to refer to objectivists and the feminine one to refer to relativists) is incapable of entertaining "any alternate structure of conceptions of what he calls 'truth'" (113). When confronted by the alternate descriptions of the relativist, the objectivist accuses her of self-refutation not because, according to Smith, self-refutation is a danger in all logical assertion but because the objectivist cannot think his way out of his own description and so forces the relativist to exist under it. Objectivism is a mode of thought that cannot conceive of thinking otherwise, whereas relativism is a mode of thought that easily thinks not only otherwise but other than otherwise. In short, the relativist can understand the objectivist, but he cannot understand her.

Smith never makes it clear why this enormous difference between the mental capacities of objectivists and relativists exists. But her claims appear to be based, as in White, on soft psychology. Smith is given to describing the objectivist in terms of his personality and emotional traits. He is a closet totalitarian: oppressive, authoritarian, compulsive, rigid, uncompromising, and, most important, anxious. Indeed, the objectivist's view of relativism is the nightmare of objectivism. Smith calls it "a phantom heresy dreamt by anxious orthodoxy under siege" (151). It is perhaps a strange twist to describe the objectivist as anxious and dogmatic at the same time, since anxiety has often been associated with the alienated consciousness of those who can no longer accept traditional beliefs. Anxiety would seem to be an emotion pro-

[15] References are to Barbara Herrnstein Smith, *Contingencies of Value: Alternate Perspectives for Critical Theory* (Cambridge, Mass.: Harvard University Press, 1988).

duced by hyperawareness, and a critic such as Harold Bloom certainly uses it in this manner when he describes the emotional traumas experienced by poets too conscious of their creative debt to precursors. Nietzsche similarly associates anxiety with the man of resentment, whose reactive concentration on his own inferiority with regard to others reveals a pathetically weak and morbid self-consciousness. But Freudian psychology does give such descriptions a certain potency when it presents the idea of the reaction formation, in which individuals confronted by their own weaknesses buttress themselves against them by withdrawing into rigid and conventional patterns of thought; and Smith seems to be relying on this model. It is a model of psychological health and illness, and clearly Smith numbers herself among the healthy.

But this healthy ability to assimilate traditional positions and to think in ways that objectivists cannot produces some bizarre identifications on Smith's part. She opens *Contingencies of Value* with a parable about Shakespeare's sonnets. It is a personal story about her inability to evaluate the sonnets, but what she reveals about herself tends to give a strange twist to her privileging of thinking otherwise. Rather than providing an account of how the sonnets have been evaluated in literary history, she tells the story of her own experience with them, and this story reveals a "special case" (5). Smith claims that she cannot evaluate Shakespeare's sonnets because she knows them too well. Although assessments of art are often connected to our experience of it, Smith argues that this experience "also batters, scars, individualizes, and specializes us" (5). "To evaluate a work of art is," she writes, "among other things, to estimate its potential value for others; but while our ability to make that estimation correctly certainly increases in time with our general and specific knowledge, it also decreases in time as we become less and less *like* anyone else, and thus less able to predict anyone else's responses on the basis of our own" (5; Smith's emphasis). I certainly do not want to accuse Smith of contradicting herself, and thus fall into narrow objectivist criteria, but it does seem puzzling to suggest that relativists grow less able to free themselves from their own descriptions as they gain more experience with description.

Becoming less and less like anyone else, however, does not preclude becoming more and more like someone in particular. For Smith moves to identify her expert experience of the sonnets with that of Shakespeare himself. There have been times, she confesses about the sonnets, "when I believed I had written them myself"; continuing in this vein, she tells how she recites from certain sonnets in the classroom only to discover that she has made them up (5–6). Smith's parable, which she calls a "monstrous piece of immodesty," transforms her not into Shakespeare's sister but into the Bard himself (9). It seems that the objectivist's inability to identify with others has a distinct disadvantage for ego development, whereas the relativist uncovers to great effect the alienated mastery of her own genius in the greatest canonical figure in literary history. For a thinker who celebrates the contingency of value and exposes its involvement in self-interest and ego anxiety, the discovery of Shakespeare as soul mate is a remarkable accident. It just shows how lucky one can be!

I began this reading of skeptical criticism by discussing Foucault's last work on sexuality because it suggests that a skepticism about categories such as the self as well as the philosophical exercise of thinking otherwise ultimately belong to some kind of hermeneutics of the self in which the goal is to oppose thought to itself. The representations of reality, axiology, and subjectivity in both White and Smith reveal the paradoxes as well as the political and ethical deficiencies of this psychological drama. The attempt to reach the most skeptical position about reality or axiology ends by affirming the existence of the self, an irony nevertheless being that this self is incompatible with the reality and values with which it must live; and thus we must speak of something like an attitude that works toward creating the conditions of the death of the self as the greatest exercise of self-mastery.[16]

White, we saw, outlines a view of unconstructed reality, while affirming that the greatest human desire is for narrative order. He therefore conceives of reality from a position radically opposed to the nature of human desire as he defines it and then moves to situate human

[16] On the current scene, the critic best associated with this tactic is Paul de Man. See chapter 4 for a detailed analysis of how de Man translates self-mourning into self-mastery.

beings with this desire in the environment most hostile to them. Politically and ethically, this position smacks of the ethic of servitude and sacrifice found in both Christian ascesis and militant reactionary politics. Similarly, the skeptical project of thinking otherwise drives Smith, in spite of herself (and here spite against the self is the dominant trope), into association with political positions that do not look as radical as her literary theories. Smith establishes a version of thought in which understanding first defeats itself and then recuperates itself as elitist. She begins by identifying with a sympathetic, relativistic position, defined as capable of understanding others, but this same talent exposes her to too much experience, and she emerges battered, scarred, individualized, and unable to understand anyone else, except the powerful, isolated, and charismatic figure of Shakespeare. It appears, in both cases, that skepticism enacts a hermeneutics of the self, in which the attempt to think otherwise culminates in the apotheosis of thought. The skeptical self achieves its deification by constantly stripping itself of poorer versions of thought, soaring toward a height that can have no groundings in history, politics, ethics, material conditions, fiction, selfhood, gender, sexuality, or any other constructions of belief. The result of doubting the false consciousness of traditional beliefs is an entity, an "Other" of thought, that is radically nonhistorical and noncontingent, this being in the case of White and Smith no mere instance of self-refutation but the fulfillment of the aberrant desire to think otherwise in the most successful and fantastic terms.

Lest my argument thus far be misunderstood for something that it is not, let me oppose myself to two possible explanations of this hermeneutics of the self. First, I am not claiming that the skeptical project of thinking otherwise produces an Other of thought because it falls prey to an unconscious process by which repressed ideas return to take control of the conscious mind. It may well be the case in any one thinker that specific unconscious material determines that certain versions of the self return even as that self is being denied; but I do not believe that this is a universal effect demonstrated by a general psychological theory such as psychoanalysis. Second, I am not arguing, à la Paul de Man, that insight in language is purchased at the cost of blindness. It may well be that thinking about one topic excludes thought about another. It may well be that some topics are related in such a fashion that insights about them necessitate blindness about others. But it is unlikely that the major terms of an argument always cancel out one another. Thought is neither so coherent nor so incoherent as to obey such laws. De Man's argument translates a psychoanalytic view of the unconscious into linguistic terms and applies its logic to philosophical rhetoric. In this sense, it is true, despite Derrida's claims to the contrary, that deconstruction is a psychoanalysis of philosophy, and consequently its greatest successes in linguistic analysis always return us to the hermeneutics of the self.[17]

How, then, does one explain these effects? It may be the case that no universal theory will account for them, and I am not even sure that one should dare to say that these effects always characterize the skeptical project. The general tendency among theorists skeptical about explanations at moments like this is to turn to the vocabulary of war, invoking "strategies," "tactics," and "maneuvers." The belief is that general statements made under such descriptions are less essentialistic; but, in fact, the only thing strategic about such terminology remains that it comes about to conceal its resemblance to theory as usual. Because they destroy with one hand what they build with the other, or mark off their beliefs as beliefs, skeptics think that they have avoided generalities and mistakes in thinking, but such strategies work only in theory, and so in theory they continue to be used. Another possible avenue for explaining such effects is to push current theories of cultural studies to their limits and begin to write the histories of thinkers and their contexts, for example, with respect to parentage, nationality, geographical enclave, education, movement, gender, race, class, and so forth. Thus, to understand the literary theories of Gayatri Spivak, one would begin by writing her psychobiography in terms of the old rules of "race, milieu, moment." It is more than mildly amusing to consider that we live in a world in which Hyppolite Taine could be seen as the most radical expression of literary theory.

Since neither of these alternatives strikes me as either honest or

[17] I refer to Derrida's opening disavowal (might we say *Verneinung?*), in "Freud and the Scene of Writing," in his *Writing and Difference,* trans. Alan Bass (Chicago: University of Chicago Press, 1978), 196, that his methods have any relation to psychoanalysis.

tasteful, my tendency is to return to ethical and political analyses of various ideas to consider why certain subject positions are developed and occupied. If this means hovering at a level of dangerous generality, I accept this situation as the price that we must pay to avoid getting even more personal about people. (I have been too personal above, and I will be too personal again; it is inevitable when one discusses the ethics and politics of someone's theories, but there are ways to mitigate the effect.) Indeed, the most ethical aspect of theory may be that its love of generality avoids doing personal violence to human beings. The intentional fallacy, if it has any value today, has at least this going for it, and no doubt poet-critics such as T. S. Eliot were well aware of this value when they first developed the idea of poetic impersonality.

Let me conclude, then, by turning to a specific description of subjectivity, which I will advance as an example of the skeptical view and use to analyze some of its general ethical and political motivations. Just to make things interesting, however, I will discuss a theory that appears at first glance to be opposed to the skeptical project of thinking otherwise because it describes selfhood not in terms of contrary thoughts but in terms of the desire to vanquish the self altogether. Bear two questions in mind in what follows: What is the self that we should want to be free of it? Who is it that desires this freedom?

As early as *Baudelaire and Freud* (1977), Leo Bersani proposed a model of the fragmented and mobile self whose desire finds its greatest fulfillment not in self-mastery but in self-shattering.[18] If the skeptical self as we know it rises toward increasing heights of self-mastery (and political correctness) by exercising an ascesis in which thought purifies itself, Bersani's version of the self takes another route by giving itself over to sexuality. "Sexuality," Bersani argues, "would be that which is intolerable to the structured self" (77). Sexuality is the experience of excess, where pleasure and pain become indistinguishable, and the self tends to fear this experience rather than to exploit its potential for explosive displacement. From the self's point of view, the experience of intense sexuality (*jouissance*) constitutes a "degrading openness" in which the self dissipates its integrity, goes outside of itself, prostitutes

[18] References are to Leo Bersani, *Baudelaire and Freud* (Berkeley and Los Angeles: University of California Press, 1977).

itself, and allows itself to be invaded and penetrated (9–10). This is why, Bersani surmises, people do not really "like" sexual pleasure, even though they may be said to enjoy it immensely.

Whereas the skeptical self desires to make its thinking more perfect, the self of *jouissance* desires to discard the self. The first is an ascesis as traditionally defined, but sexuality becomes for Bersani another mode of ascesis by which the self "spiritualizes itself" (32). This spiritualization cannot be understood in terms of either abstraction or sensation. Indeed, it is a voracious irony to use the term "spiritualization," and the fact that Bersani uses it reveals that he is deliberately questioning what we usually mean by purity. According to him, sex by its very intensity propels the self beyond abstraction and sensation, shattering "epistemological securities and ontological boundaries" and plunging the ego into the experience of a "noncentered floating of unanchored partial selves" (67–68). In other words, intense pleasure and pain free the self from itself and from the meanings that confine it. Differences associated with the order of personality, physical boundaries, gender, race, class, and linguistic hierarchies are disrupted and displaced.

But why is it important to get rid of the self and these hierarchies? In the early *Baudelaire and Freud*, Bersani sometimes mentions that sexual pleasure brings together the worlds of the sadist and the masochist. The ironic climate of Baudelaire's prose poems is in fact a meeting of these two opposing worldviews, for Bersani explains that "violence in the prose poems is simultaneously seen and repudiated" (128). When Bersani turns, in a later essay on AIDS, to the sadomasochistic theater of the gay-macho style, however, the significance of violence to his theory of sexuality emerges with greater clarity.[19] The essay on AIDS situates Bersani's ideas in an ethical and political setting, and we begin to see why he wishes to discard the self. He describes gay sexual practices in terms of the opposition between ego and pleasure, in which sexuality moves between a hyperbolic sense of the self and a loss of all consciousness of the self. In the former, gay sex resembles heterosexuality and its tendency to placate the ego by affirming the natural authority of one person over the other. The desire to penetrate in gay

[19] References are to Leo Bersani, "Is the Rectum a Grave?," *AIDS: Cultural Analysis, Cultural Activism,* ed. Douglas Crimp (Cambridge, Mass.: MIT Press, 1988), 197–222.

as well as in heterosexual practices springs from a lust to dominate, and it exposes the self's need to divert pleasure to win authority. Bersani calls this type of ambition a "salvational project" designed to preserve us from sexual intensities and a "kind of selfless communication with 'lower' orders of being" (221). In the latter experience of sexuality, sexual pleasure displaces the authority of the self, opening it up to the vertiginous possibility of selfless communication. *Jouissance* strips away lust for power and violence, eradicating the hierarchies that institutionalize aggression and cruelty.

In other words, the politics and ethics of the gay-macho style do not lie in its specific relation to existing institutional norms and laws. Bersani discards the political and moral folklore, the "system of gliding emphases," by which homosexual practices in general have become associated with radical politics (206). In his view, gay sex is not in itself a protest against either right-wing politics or conservative heterosexual practices. It is not a form of "'semiotic guerilla warfare' waged by sexual outsiders against the dominant order" (207). In fact, gay practices are as susceptible to rank, hierarchy, and competition as any other. But in Bersani's view these practices do nevertheless possess a special ethical and political power with regard to human psychology—the originary site of the constitution of ethics and politics—because they have the potential to free us of the ego structures that distort interpersonal relations. In marriage and other long-term relationships, Bersani explains, our heads get in the way of our pleasure, and love relations degenerate into a series of unending quarrels and power plays. But promiscuous and spontaneous sexual relations do not permit the fixation of the self necessary to fuel power and conflict. Rather, these practices discard the self to have sex. Bersani is emphatic in his condemnation of the self as the source of violence. He calls selfhood a "sacrosanct value" that "accounts for human beings' extraordinary willingness to kill in order to protect the seriousness of their statements," and he views the self as a "practical convenience; promoted to the status of an ethical ideal, it is a sanction for violence" (222). Gay sexual practices hold the possibility of an intense sexual pleasure that breaks down the kinds of differences responsible for such violence.

They invent another ethics, one that represents *"jouissance* as a mode of ascesis" (222).

Although Bersani's theory of the self may seem at odds with that implied by other skeptical critics, it shares many of the same premises, and its language is not so different in the final analysis. Skeptical critics view the self in terms of constructions that must be cast off in order to think more correctly. Their motivation for this strategy is ethical and political because they associate the constructions of false belief with social inequities and violence. Bersani makes these same points with a vengeance. For him, thinking otherwise ventures to the far reaches of thinking toward the Other of thought, the unconscious. Unlike the more typical skeptical critic, who desires a hyperawareness in order to avoid immoralities, Bersani desires to plunge the self into unconsciousness, but the superego of the skeptic shares the same motivations as the unconscious for Bersani, if only because he views the unconscious as the ethical domain par excellence: the ethical in Bersani as in the majority of his contemporaries refers to the possibility of nonviolence and social equality. Jubilant sexuality translates instantly into ecstatic politics because the openness of *jouissance* creates the oceanic sensation of being in a free and loving polis. To think otherwise is to open oneself to others, to swim among them in unbounded communion. The killing of the self with sexual pleasure means for Bersani its sacrifice to a community of others.

I will not become entangled in the question of whether Bersani's politics are conservative or radical.[20] It may be characteristic of his

[20] As I write this introduction, the war with Iraq has reached its sixth day. Last night on the "ABC Evening News," the human interest story focused on a marine general giving his troops a pep talk for battle. He asked why marines fight and have always fought. The answer was not that they are fighting for America, apple pie, or their hometown. They fight out of love. Like the mother who finds the strength to lift a car off her child, the marine finds the inner strength to jump on a grenade, sacrificing himself to save his friends. "The marine," the general insisted, "fights for his buddies." He sacrifices himself in battle for his fellow marines. I relate this anecdote not to insist on the so-called homosocial nature of military organizations but to suggest how strange are the correspondences between conservative and radical arguments. Bersani's homosexual ascesis mirrors the philosophy expressed by the general, but it is unlikely that the U.S. Marine Corps would appreciate it.

conflation of differences that this question becomes difficult to answer; and he himself is well aware of the dangers of using political labels in a cross fire between separate areas of description. But the difficulty in describing Bersani's position is not merely the by-product of his sexual politics. It arises as well because Bersani espouses the logic of skepticism, which, although it may describe itself as radical, turns reactionary in its response to dogmatism. It is therefore important to my argument to make sure that his theories are accepted as an example of skeptical criticism and not seen as a maverick position of some kind.

Here the key is to ask from where the desire to eradicate the self emerges. In other words, who or what wants to get rid of the self? Is it the self that desires to strip itself of its own immoral authority? Or is it the unconscious that wishes to impose its ethical vision on the self? These questions expose Bersani's skeptical credentials because they show that he relies on the existence of the same type of oppositionality that compelled Kant to create his critical philosophy. The self and the unconscious occupy separate spheres for Bersani.[21] He cannot conceive of either the self or the unconscious as responsible for both the desire for coherence and the desire for incoherence. Rather, the self is the domain of orthodoxy and dogmatism, of the grounds in short, against which the unconscious is to be defined. By definition, *jouissance* has no grounds; it is, to repeat Bersani, "a noncentered floating of unanchored partial selves." The distinction between the self and the unconscious thereby enacts the drama of the skeptical self, in which it struggles against false consciousness and the dangerous constructions of belief in order to purify itself. The irony is, of course, that when Bersani does come up with a formulation that breaks down the traditional opposition between skepticism and dogmatism, it is not a result of his theory. That the ethics and politics of *jouissance* reproduce the traditional vision of social communion that radical skepticism finds so confining mixes up the historical differences between the radical and the reactionary, the skeptical and the dogmatic, and the ego and the id; but Bersani's theory neither predicts nor explains this fusion. The moral enters his theory from the outside in the form of a bald assertion,

[21] In chapter 2 I will call such formations a philosophical version of the Truman Doctrine.

an assertion of the types of ideals and fantasies that skepticism and dogmatism secretly share.[22] Bersani's notion of *jouissance* appears to be a refusal of self-mastery, but it ends by inserting itself into the traditional project of skeptical ascesis.

The formation of beliefs is fundamental to the way that human beings direct their lives and actions. Truth and falsehood are best seen as properties of beliefs in relation to the purposes for which we form beliefs in the first place—that is, the goals for which we live and act— and these goals are a function of the interests that move us. Truth and falsehood presuppose, as a result, not only our beliefs as their primary context but also the phenomena of interests, goals, and purposeful actions. Social existence depends on the tautology of belief in which our actions and ideas are risked, and politics is defined as that domain in which beliefs determine the interests, purposes, and actions that lead to these same beliefs, which explains why political choices are always dangerous, and necessarily so. To adopt a resolute skepticism toward beliefs—to label them arbitrary constructions—is to move outside the hermeneutic circle of belief, the tautology, in which politics takes place. It is to abandon our "home in the world," as Hannah Arendt called it, in the name of the higher but dubious reality of a politically independent truth. It is in the end to court the ultimate mastery of defining our existence independently of the dangerous political and ethical world.

We may wish to abandon belief for the best of all possible reasons— for example, to avoid the violence of belief—but skeptics cannot live outside the risky tautology of belief any more than ordinary mortals can. Skepticism can never be the philosophical basis of a politics, and when skeptics strip themselves of founding beliefs they only deprive themselves of political direction. This explains in part why proponents of radical hermeneutics are sometimes tossed in the direction of reactionary politics: hermeneutic skepticism leaves criticism without the

---

[22] The corollary of Bersani's acceptance of the traditional ethic of social communion is his idea that the gay man demolishes his uncontrollable identification with reactionary and murderous judgments against him at the moment when he opens himself in the act of anal intercourse to bury the symbol of this murderous judgment, the phallus, in his rectum (222).

orienting beliefs necessary to direct its politics. Rather, the political craft defines itself on the basis of the beliefs and directions that it chooses to affirm, and to renounce this choice for the sake of logical purity, harmony, nonviolence, or personal ascesis ends by exposing one to arbitrariness in the very domain where it is most perilous: the realm of political practice.

The skeptical project dreams of mastery by opposing itself to "false" groundings and constructions of thought, be they called "the self," "truth," "authority," "value," "violence," "reality," or simply "belief." It makes a virtue of thinking otherwise without thinking about the directions in which it may lead. Often, this project does arrive at a genuinely critical understanding of the dogmatic aspects of the categories and institutions by which the history of ethics and politics has proceeded, and herein lies its great value. But, just as often, it ends in the irony of saying one thing and meaning something else, where the "something else" recovers not the skeptical insights of thinking otherwise or an immaculate and radical alterity but the categories, conventions, and traditions against which skeptics desire so ardently to oppose themselves. This suggests that the skeptical wish to think otherwise about ourselves is akin to those dreams of family romance in which the children of the poor fantasize about having wealthy and noble parents. But we who are destined to another poverty—the intellectual poverty defined by the limits of our ability to think our way out of every ethical, political, and philosophical dilemma—may wish to make the transition from the pleasure of fantasy to the possibility of finding a home in the world, and so direct our efforts not to the dream of thinking otherwise but to the modest task of thinking about how we do think about others and ourselves.

2

Cold War Criticism

The cold war era began officially with Churchill's "Iron Curtain" speech in March 1946, and until recently it was believed to have ended with the fall of the Berlin Wall in November 1989. The failed Soviet coup of August 1991 revised this history, but the events confirmed for many what had been the unspoken truth of the cold war era: the history of the cold war is in part a history of false endings. When Gorbachev was temporarily deposed on the morning of the nineteenth, every conservative politician in Washington and some of the liberal ones found themselves thinking that glasnost and arms reduction had proceeded too swiftly, and after the coup failed the experts debated over whether nuclear forces had for sixty-three hours fallen into the hands of the communist hard-liners.

We are afraid that the cold war will never end, and so the history of the cold war is the story of our skepticism about endings, intentions, interpretations, and calculations concerning numbers, troop movements, weapons, negotiations, and claims to truth and falsehood. We are forever watchful and on our guard. Our fear contributes an essential part to the cold war mentality. It determines the distrust, suspicion, paranoia, and skepticism that have always characterized the cold war era. We have seen the cold war come and go so many times that we must recognize that one defining feature of the cold war era is not knowing where we stand in relation to our enemies or friends, whichever the case may be at the moment. It is a state that requires skepticism, and this skepticism in turn preserves the state. This is the cold war effect.

This image of the cold war is largely uncontroversial, acceptable to reactionary and radical thinkers alike—although each party has made use of it for different ends. More controversial, although less important, is the idea that modern criticism has been powerfully influenced on all sides by the cold war, especially because historians of literary criticism have not yet examined this influence with any kind of rigor. Modern criticism has its roots in the philosophies of Aristotle and Kant and in the line of poet-critics stretching from Coleridge through Eliot, but the form of academic criticism that has come increasingly to be identified as "modern" emerged with the New Criticism. The New Criticism appeared in the 1920s and 1930s, but it is most associated with the postwar world, when it acquired an institutional status with the help of the postwar boom in population and education. Those texts most frequently anthologized as examples of the New Criticism and from which its basic principles are drawn appeared in the first years of the cold war. "The Intentional Fallacy" and "The Affective Fallacy" by Wimsatt and Beardsley were published in 1946 and 1949. Cleanth Brooks's *The Well Wrought Urn,* which includes both "The Language of Paradox" and "The Heresy of Paraphrase," came out in 1947, and two years later Brooks published "Irony as a Principle of Structure." Modern criticism is a product of the cold war, and the repeated emphasis by the New Critics on objectivity, ambiguity, paradox, the impossibility of paraphrase, and double meaning are part of the cold war climate.

When John Crowe Ransom turned in his 1941 essay "Criticism as Pure Speculation" to a "political way of thinking," he gave the rationale for both a new method of interpretation and a new kind of curriculum, but he also revealed an obvious fact about modern criticism and its politics. Here he describes poetry as a democratic state and prose as a totalitarian one:

> A poem is, so to speak, a democratic state, whereas a prose discourse—mathematical, scientific, ethical, or practical and vernac-

ular—is a totalitarian state. The intention of a democratic state is to perform the work of state as effectively as it can perform it, subject to one reservation of conscience: that it will not despoil its members, the citizens, of the free exercise of their own private and independent characters. But the totalitarian state is interested solely in being effective, and regards the citizens as no citizens at all; that is, regards them as functional members whose existence is totally defined by their allotted contributions to its ends; it has no use for their private characters, and therefore no provision for them. I indicate of course the extreme or polar opposition between two polities, without denying that a polity may come to us rather mixed up.

In this trope the operation of the state as a whole represents of course the logical paraphrase or argument of the poem. The private character of the citizens represents the particularity asserted by the parts in the poem. . . . A poem is a *logical structure* having a *local texture*. (Ransom's emphases)[1]

In the ideal of the "concrete universal," which Ransom is in fact elaborating here, the New Critics found the symbolic means by which universality and particularity might be combined and given mutual respect and by which two opposing political philosophies might find their natural hierarchy and heal their divisions. Only in the new republic of poetry could the "logical structure" of universal principles (law) and the freedom of the "local texture" (the private citizen) exist without conflict. The New Critics quickly established a canon of poetry to found the new republic in which a purer democracy would defeat totalitarianism and bring an end to the cold war. At first they shunned the poetry of the romantics, whose supposed sentimentality, egotism, and alienation had led them into emotional license and to the prosification of poetry. The New Critics turned instead to the metaphysical poets, for whom ambiguity and paradox formed the basis of a "unified sensibility" and whose age, characterized by antagonistic religious ideologies, political distrust, and skepticism, bore some resemblance to the cold war era. Eventually they turned to the romantic poets, but they contrived to read them as if they were metaphysical: romantic poetry became paradoxical, ironic, and ambiguous. Indeed,

[1] John Crowe Ransom, "Criticism as Pure Speculation," in *The Intent of the Critic*, ed. Donald A. Stauffer (Princeton, N.J.: Princeton University Press, 1941), 91–124, esp. 108–10.

American deconstruction, continuing this legacy, has now made it almost impossible to conceive of any form of poetry that might lack the virtues of indeterminacy, irony, and paradox, and with the recognition that these virtues characterize prose as well, the totalitarian principle has been effectively banned from the republic of letters.[2]

While critics have from early on worked enthusiastically to represent literary form as the condition of a moral and democratic world, in effect rewriting Kant's famous dictum about beauty and morality in terms of literature and politics, they have only of late brought the same enthusiasm to bear on canon formation. Poetry symbolized for Ransom and the New Critics an ideal polity in which distinct particulars exist in harmonious and egalitarian relation under the conditions of law. Poststructualist theorists have extended this view of individual works to the concept of the canon. The idea is to view the polity of the canon in the same light as the republic of a given poem, thereby reducing conflict and establishing peaceful coexistence. The formation of the canon is no idle business, according to cold war critics, for it provides an ethical barometer indicating the health or sickness of our political systems. Too much sameness risks the resurgence of the sickly totalitarian principle. A multitude of differences indicates healthy democracy.

Consequently, canon formation has become one battleground on which cold war fears are played out. Each canon supposedly protects an ideological interest, making it necessary to approach canon formation with the cold war virtues of disbelief, distrust, and general suspicion. "Canons are," according to the current view, "simply ideological banners for social groups."[3] Nevertheless, skeptical critics have always proposed new canons, and these new canons do not change one iota the political symbolism that canon formation has always served. It is

---

[2] J. Hillis Miller, in *The Ethics of Reading* (New York: Columbia University Press, 1987), has elaborated a method based entirely on indeterminacy in which ethics consists in letting prose be ambiguous and in letting the ambiguity of prose be.

[3] Charles Altieri, *Canon and Consequences: Reflections on the Ethical Force of Imaginative Ideals* (Evanston, Ill.: Northwestern University Press, 1990), 23. Altieri makes a strong case against the skepticism motivating canon reform, while acknowledging the ethical principles of the reformists.

an irony that the "great books" curriculum now being attacked as undemocratic and totalitarian was conceived during World War II largely in order to ensure the survival of democratic ideals. Skeptics as well as traditionalists use canon formation to activate literature as a social force in order to provide the ideal polity upon which a better society might be built. The first impulse in canon formation is always a skeptical one. Because we dislike the existing world we form new canons in the hope of possessing the symbols necessary to build a revolutionary new world.

But a danger exists in seeing skepticism as a sufficient explanation for either literary works or politics. We come to prefer the purity of our skepticism to the chaos of the political world, and no form of politics can ever measure up to our fantasy. Canon formation has become a domain in which skepticism about real politics makes way for a utopian view in which politics has become unnecessary. It is as if the orderly arrangement of different kinds of texts in the canon miraculously puts an end to the differences that each represents, and all live happily ever after in peace and harmony. Here is a world, a dream world, where political differences, choices, sacrifices, and mistakes do not exist. Because politics is so often designed to reduce conflict, it is too often seen as the source of conflict, and especially in a cold war context politics has come to symbolize what divides people. Is not the ideal political world one where politics does not exist? Has not the greatest dream of politics always been to rid itself of politics? The cold war's version of this principle is: given the requisite amount of distrust, distrust will outlive its usefulness.

Cold war criticism perpetuates a mentality that overestimates our tendency to miscalculate, and it thinks the worst of other people's interpretations and intentions—if it considers their intentions at all. It is suspicious of emotions, claims for morality, and altruism. The new historicism's critique of power, Lyotard's idea of the *différend*, Lacan's attack on altruism, and Foucault's analysis of micropower translate cold war suspicions into critical skepticism. The widespread critical idea that interpretation and theory are acts of violence obeys the same impulse. W. J. T. Mitchell, for example, introduces a widely read anthology called *The Politics of Interpretation* by asking the reader to substitute the notion of "interpretation" for "war" in a passage drawn from Clausewitz, thereby expressing the cold war belief that war must be waged according to a grammar of skillful tactics, bold lies, and distorted truths. Paul de Man wonders whether his own method, which he calls "totalizing," is not also guilty of "totalitarianism." J. Hillis Miller reduces the ethics of Kant to the word *Achtung,* now a kitschy embodiment of Nazi brutality, having been spoken by a thousand actors in the war dramas produced by Hollywood during and after World War II. Jacques Derrida rewrites the structuralism of Jean Rousset's *Forme et signification* in terms of "Force and Significance," accuses Foucault of running "the risk of being totalitarian," and discovers in his own concept of deconstruction an apocalyptic vision of the nuclear age.[4]

Modern criticism has made a virtue of cold war paranoia. It redraws the character of the critical consciousness by focusing it inward toward the violent side of its better hopes. That cold war criticism has introduced a model of the self-conscious critic whose greatest desire is to deny his or her own agency in the world shows that modern criticism is tied to our vision of what the World Wars and the postwar era have taught us about the darker nature of human beings. The desire to escape from the self promoted everywhere in cold war criticism obeys the desire to have a self other than the one revealed to us by the horrors of the twentieth century.[5] This view may seem Nietzschean and thus to predate the cold war era, but the philosophy of Nietzsche cannot be thought apart from its appropriation by the Nazis. Cold war criticism's embrace of Nietzsche is only another way to symbolize its fear

[4] See, respectively: W. J. T. Mitchell, ed., *The Politics of Interpretation* (Chicago: University of Chicago Press, 1983), 1; Paul de Man, *The Resistance to Theory* (Minneapolis: University of Minnesota Press, 1986), 19; J. Hillis Miller, *The Ethics of Reading* (New York: Columbia University Press, 1987), 19–23; Jacques Derrida, *Writing and Difference,* trans. Alan Bass (Chicago: University of Chicago Press, 1978), 3–5, 57, and his article "No Apocalypse, Not Now," *Diacritics* 14, no. 2 (1984): 20–31. In *The Ethics of Criticism* (Ithaca, N.Y.: Cornell University Press, 1988) I analyzed in great detail the attitudes of modern critics toward violence, but I did not at the time make a connection to the cold war era.

[5] Jacques Lacan, for example, has called existentialism a concentration-camp criticism, but he seems oblivious to the probability that his own critique of altruism issues from the same political environment; see chap. 7, esp. n.3.

that we have become our own worst enemies. Small wonder that self-hood is subject to such vicious attacks.

Cold war critics use literature and other aesthetic forms to symbolize the harmony and order that they believe have become impossible to find in the postwar world. We are attracted to formalism because we see the mirror image of our own distraught and disordered condition in the perfections of pure form. Certainly, the cold war era is not the first period in history when literature has been used to represent a better ethical and political world. The aesthetic symbolism of Kant, Schiller, Wordsworth, and Shelley comes easily to mind as historical precedents. But the cold war period has produced some of history's most political and ethical critics, perhaps for the reason that criticism has itself reached a critical mass in this age of the Bomb.

I want to propose more than a metaphor to consider the political orientation of postwar criticism, although the metaphorical dimension should not be underestimated. Metaphors provide the symbolism by which critics express their ethics and politics, and this symbolism allows them the appearance of engaging with the world scene, while in reality avoiding its disorder and violence. Rather, I am claiming that the cold war context of modern criticism provides the key to understanding many of its theoretical developments, political stances, ethical claims, and psychological attitudes. It is easy to believe that "conflict of interpretations" is merely about validity in interpretation or about small academic squabbles because it so often is. The academic world is tragic in its smallness and comic in its aspirations. It believes that it can insulate itself from the world and change the world at the same time. But debates about conflict of interpretations reveal that conflict has more than a local meaning; conflict is a major theme of modern criticism because it has been the major preoccupation of the postwar era. In the conflict of interpretations is revealed not merely a war of words but a general attitude toward violence and disagreement, an attitude to which the cold war mentality has made an elementary and formative contribution.

I hope that it begins to grow clear that the real context of the so-called conflict of interpretations is the cold war era and that modern criticism is a cold war criticism. I would like to explore this context in

greater detail both historically and metaphorically.[6] Part of my intention will be to locate expressions of distrust, suspicion, paranoia, and
skepticism in their proper cold war setting, and I will also address the
evolution of the cold war era as registered by the succession of critical
fashions. As we move from the era of strong leadership (Hitler, Stalin,
FDR, and Churchill), through the age of propaganda (wariness about
the military-industrial complex, obsessions about espionage and infiltration in government, and fears about brainwashing in the arts, especially in Hollywood), and finally to the era of superpowers (Star Wars
defenses and nuclear disarmament), cold war criticism, always one
step behind events, expresses its anxieties in terms of the analogies of
affective criticism (charisma, emotion, feeling, self-control, unified sensibility), of language (self-reflexivity, self-deconstruction, aporia, indeterminacy), and of power (history, ideology, economics, technologies
of the self and society). Old fears are not left behind with the creation
of new analogies, and these analogies have their own histories, but it is
possible to see a definite trend in the way that criticism expresses cold

[6] I need at the outset to make several introductory points about the material that I will be
examining and about my approach to it. I will be reading three works: "The Affective
Fallacy" (1949) by Wimsatt and Beardsley, Geoffrey Hartman's *Criticism in the
Wilderness* (1980), and Stephen Greenblatt's *Shakespearean Negotiations* (1988). I
have not chosen these texts because they are extreme examples of any one point of view.
In fact, they are remarkably diverse, characterized more by a spirit of arbitration than by
the desire to be radical, for each may be said to mediate between radical theories and a
conservative audience. All three writings possess a heterogeneous quality, containing
more ideas and positions than I would ideally desire, if my motivation were proof rather
than suggestion.

Parenthetical references are to W. K. Wimsatt and Monroe Beardsley, "The Affective
Fallacy," in W. K. Wimsatt, *The Verbal Icon: Studies in the Meaning of Poetry*
(Lexington: University of Kentucky Press, 1954), 20–39; Geoffrey H. Hartman, *Criti-
cism in the Wilderness: The Study of Literature Today* (New Haven, Conn.: Yale
University Press, 1980); and Stephen Greenblatt, *Renaissance Self-Fashioning: From
Moore to Shakespeare* (Chicago: University of Chicago Press, 1980), *Shakespearean
Negotiations: The Circulation of Social Energy in Renaissance England* (Berkeley and
Los Angeles: University of California Press, 1988), and *Learning to Curse: Essays in
Early Modern Culture* (New York: Routledge, 1990).

For the history of the postwar era, I have relied on Roy Douglas, *From War to Cold
War, 1942–48* (New York: Macmillan, 1981); Ralph Levering, *The Cold War 1945–
1987*, 2d ed. (Arlington Heights. Ill.: Harlan Davidson, 1988 [1982]); and John
Sharnik, *Inside the Cold War: An Oral History* (New York: Arbor House, 1987).

war anxieties and conflicts over the years. Finally, another part of my intention will be to suggest that the cold war mentality in criticism, while well-meaning and often ethically motivated, fails to escape the very context against which it designs its every purpose.[7] It also fails to provide an adequate account of the nature of politics and literature. We need to resist it if we are going to move beyond the cold war era toward a different view of the world, politics, and literature.

Art Is a Cold Sphere

Over the years "The Affective Fallacy" (1949) has come to stand with "The Intentional Fallacy" (1946) as the two guarantors of the New Critical belief in poetic autonomy. The intentional fallacy remains largely in force today because poststructuralist theories have as little use for the self as the New Criticism did for the poet. The affective fallacy, however, possesses little influence at present as a critical doctrine. Reader-response criticism launched an early attack against the essay, and today few people are willing to say that the reader and reading are not important dimensions of interpretation. The effect has been to discount "The Affective Fallacy" as an attack on the importance of the reader, but the essay in fact has only a little to do with this issue.

Ransom inaugurated the New Critical project by trying to escape from the affective terms of Eliot's theories, and his embrace of the "paraphrasable core" of poetry attempts to place the criticism of poetry on a logical and objective basis without, however, denying that emotions are important. Wimsatt and Beardsley, although skeptical of Ransom's views to some degree, follow the same agenda in "The Affective Fallacy." The problem with the essay, however, is that they do not confine themselves to this single agenda. One of the reasons that "The Affective Fallacy" is seldom read today—that it exists merely as a

---

[7] Skepticism is often seen as a response to the defeat of the progressive social reforms of the 1960s. But it also characterizes those cold war attitudes against which the counterculture arose, so it is hard to attribute it to so late a development. The paranoia of the sixties slogan, "Never trust anyone over thirty," sinks into cold war suspicion, when we realize that it refers to a generation of people who did not themselves trust each other.

symbol of New Critical obstinacy—is that it is in fact a very difficult
essay to read. First, it is amazingly varied in its texture—often marked
by irrelevance, irony, and wisecracks—and raises a stunning number
of questions for a large number of disciplines. Second, the essay is an
attempt to mediate between the academic literary theorists of the day
and a group of nonacademic critics who wrote for daily and monthly
publications. Wimsatt and Beardsley quote from their reading of the
New York Times and *The New Yorker,* but we have for the most part
forgotten the contexts for both their theoretical arguments and their
clippings from contemporary periodicals because they were so local
and timely. Third, the essay is a veritable catalogue of cold war conflicts and anxieties, and these emotions, found in an essay on the
subject of emotion, threaten to take command of the essay itself.[8] The
real affective fallacy has very little to do with reader response; instead,
it describes the belief that conflict of interpretations arises because of
the emotional limitations of interpreters. To eliminate conflict of interpretations, Wimsatt and Beardsley argue, it is necessary to create an
atmosphere of objectivity, self-control, and disinterestedness. The alternative is to fall prey to emotional chaos, mob psychology, soul
cultivation, mass hallucination, and charismatic leadership.

This alternative characterizes only too obviously the dangers presented by world events of the cold war period. Hitler and his hypnotic
hold on Germany were fresh in everyone's mind. Stalin and Truman
battled each other in the daily papers. The issue of the Sunday *New
York Times* for April 20, 1947, which Wimsatt and Beardsley cite in
their essay, fully illustrates the atmosphere of crisis reigning between
the Soviet Union and the United States during the spring and summer
of 1947, when the United States initiated aid to Greece and Turkey, the
president announced the Truman Doctrine, the Marshall Plan was
established, and the U.S. government first adopted a policy of "con-
tainment" toward the Soviet Union. The *New York Times* announces
the anniversary of the birth of Hitler, who would have turned fifty-

[8] As I was finishing this chapter I came across William Epstein's "Counter-Intelligence:
Cold War Criticism and Eighteenth Century Studies," *ELH* 57 (1990): 63–90. Epstein
focuses in particular on Wimsatt and Maynard Mack, arguing that the intelligence
community had strong ties to the university during the earlier years of the cold war.

three that day if he had not committed suicide, and the front page includes an article bearing the headline U.S. SLIPPING IN ATOMIC RACE in which the then chairman of the Atomic Energy Commission, David E. Lilienthal, recommends "strengthening this nation as the only remaining bulwark of democracy." The issue also reports on the attack of the "French Reds" against Truman and de Gaulle; on the split between American and Soviet policies in the Northern Tier countries of Greece, Turkey, and Iran; on George Marshall's meeting with Stalin about the Truman Doctrine; on Germany's occupation by the Big Four; on the status of buffer states between the Soviet Union and the West; and on architectural plans for the United Nations building. An entire page is devoted to Henry A. Wallace's peace mission to Great Britain and Western Europe, during which the ex–secretary of commerce, fired by Truman for urging greater cooperation with the Soviets, repeatedly attacks the Truman Doctrine and claims that American policy toward Russia is leading to a third world war. In Sweden, for example, Wallace declares that "it is time to build up a middle path of international feeling, not against Russian communism, nor against American capitalism, but for the common man's democracy." But the political cartoons accompanying his remarks picture him as a "simple Iowa farm boy" sowing "distrust of America" across Europe, and as a puppet of Stalin, "travelling by remote control."

At first glance the concerns of Wimsatt and Beardsley would seem far afield from these events. They appear to be making a series of simple critical points: emotion and impressionism are obstacles to objective criticism because they confuse the results of a poem with the poem itself, missing the fact that the goal of criticism is to understand why and how poems create certain emotional effects. When they call the affective fallacy a special case of epistemological skepticism, they seem to be making their usual plea that we pay attention to meaning as it is embodied in language rather than fall prey to bardolatry or soul-adventuring among masterpieces. These points define the critic's task around the poetic object as such. But the objections of Wimsatt and Beardsley to the affective fallacy extend beyond literary criticism, for they do not provide examples of how affective criticism goes wrong in the reading of poetry. Rather, they stress its dangers by giving examples drawn from politics. The affective fallacy emerges as the philosophical complement of allowing our emotions to run away with us. Paying attention to the facts at hand and to the nature of the facts, Wimsatt and Beardsley suggest, is the more objective and safer approach to interpreting both poetry and politics.

I do not want to discuss at length the opening attack by Wimsatt and Beardsley on the emotivism of I. A. Richards and Charles Stevenson. What is important for my purposes is to understand that Wimsatt and Beardsley wish to anchor interpretation not solely in ethical and affective relativism ("descriptive" versus "emotive meaning," "meaning" versus "suggestion," "descriptive meaning" versus "descriptive suggestion," and so forth) but in the nature of objects and events, and that their examples of objects and events derive from cold war politics. Objective criticism in their definition has to do with objects of reality, a fact that often escapes readers of the essay today because we have come to assume that the New Critical doctrine of poetic autonomy describes the poem as an order distinct from reality, when in fact it allows a strong commensurability to exist between affects in language and the objects represented by language. This means that emotive effects will be determined not only by a series of conventions governing how we relate to objects, facts, behavior, and events, but by the nature of reality itself, which determines the conventions that arise to govern interpretation in the first place. Poems become objects of emotions by reproducing the relation between objects and emotions. Or as Wimsatt and Beardsley put it, "similar emotions attach to various objects because of similarity in the objects or in their relations" (27). There exists a certain freedom in this process, but a limit to it arises in the very nature of objects and emotions.

The examples provided by Wimsatt and Beardsley both to illustrate the views of affective critics and to attack them are drawn mostly from recent political events, and even when they are not seem to be colored by them. Thus they illustrate the difference between descriptive meaning and emotive import with the two sentences: "'General X ordered the execution of 50,000 civilian hostages,' or 'General X is guilty of the murder of 50,000 civilian hostages'"(24). Or they take up the emotional effect produced when the communists appropriate the term "democracy" and apply it to their own regime. Even the difference between "liberty" and "license," which Wimsatt and Beardsley use repeatedly to exemplify the phenomenon that words having the same meaning can produce different affects, is colored by contemporary politics, since "license" is the term applied by Marxist theory to what democrats call "liberty." The catalogue of examples climaxes with an experiment designed by an emotive psychologist. To the sentence, "There should be a revolution every twenty years," the experimenter in emotive responses attaches first the name Karl Marx, arousing suspicion, and then the name Thomas Jefferson, provoking applause (25). If these example are not enough to demonstrate the political quality of the essay, I log one last illustration. To prove the importance of the objective qualities of words over their emotive effects, Wimsatt and Beardsley remark that it was not for reasons of magic but Japanese phonetics that "*lollapalooza* and *lullabye* [*sic*] were used against infiltration tactics on Guadalcanal"(25).

When applied to theories of poetic meaning, the stress placed by Wimsatt and Beardsley on the nature of objects and their referential necessities translates into the claim that the objects of poetry severely limit interpretive relativism and emotional license. The critics mean to stabilize conflict in interpretation by anchoring meaning in objects. Only the strongest epistemological skepticism could argue that it is as easy to write a romance about an onion as about a rose. "*The Romance of the Rose* could not, without loss," Wimsatt and Beardsley claim, citing C. S. Lewis, "be rewritten as *The Romance of the Onion*" (38). Nor could the murder of Duncan by Macbeth, they argue, ever be the fit subject of a Christmas carol. When confronted by the corpse of Polynices, according to Wimsatt and Beardsley, we discover a galaxy of symbols that is hardly relative or arbitrary but tied to the nature of the object itself. The point being made is, of course, that the natures of events and objects fix emotive value, and that we best understand this value by objectively analyzing how objects and poetic language are arranged in the poem. It is certainly worth stressing, however, that the galaxy of symbols evoked by Wimsatt and Beardsley contains a stunning array of wartime images: bullets, knife wounds, poison, daggers in the air, bloody hands, ancient murders, and tragedies of betrayal, of lust for power, and of fights to the death between enemy twins.

In short, although Wimsatt and Beardsley would like to provide an objective analysis of emotion, their emotions run away with them. My point is neither that Wimsatt and Beardsley succumb to the usual logical reversals revealed by deconstructive critics in recent years nor that the minor terms of their argument swallow the major ones. The central argument of the essay concerns emotion because Wimsatt and Beardsley understand its enormous power both in poetic expression and in contemporary world events. Otherwise, they would not parallel the poetic and the political so consistently. My point is, rather, a historical one about the influence of the cold war climate on literary criticism. The anxieties and fears of their day influenced the critical questions posed by Wimsatt and Beardsley, and because their topic is emotion, the conduit between criticism and politics is that much stronger. The stakes in trying to form an objective criticism were therefore especially high. The affective fallacy allows emotion to reign over the critical spirit, and Wimsatt and Beardsley feared that it would have the same effect in politics as it has had in criticism.

To understand why Wimsatt and Beardsley feared emotion, it is helpful to look at their definition of it. Part 3 of the essay is devoted to a historical reading of affective criticism, and it is here that Wimsatt and Beardsley express their greatest hesitations and fears about what emotion is and what it does. Earlier in the essay they made the following statement about emotion: "Emotion, it is true, has a well-known capacity to fortify opinion, to inflame cognition, and to grow upon itself in surprising proportions to grains of reason. We have mob psychology, psychosis, and neurosis" (26–27). Now they place this definition in a historical context. From their point of view, emotion has long held sway in the study of literature, and it has grown even stronger in modern times. They note the examples of the affective criticism of Plato, Longinus, Lipps, Tolstoy, Santayana, Max Eastman, and Richards. They remark that poets, desirous of bardolatry, have encouraged the growth of a criticism based on emotions. They finger the romantic era as a special source of the emotive style.

Their little history turns political, however, when Wimsatt and Beardsley begin to chart the importance of emotions for discipleship and leadership, in effect, turning to the topic of charisma. The soul-cultivation of romantic poets charms "young persons interested in poetry" and "introspective amateurs" (29). Nor are critics above the egotism of self-fascination. Wimsatt and Beardsley quote Anatole France's dictum that the literary critic ought to announce, "Gentleman, I am going to speak about myself apropos of Shakespeare, apropos of Racine" (29). The audience, transfixed by the charisma of the "contagious teacher," "poetic radiator," and "magnetic rhapsode," is overwhelmed and flies repeatedly to the flame of emotion to feel the heat of experience (29). Wimsatt and Beardsley attack newspaper critics for encouraging emotional reactions in readers and audiences, citing a review in the *New York Times,* in which the writer claims that "a poem means nothing to me unless it can carry me away with . . . its emotion, over the obstacles of reality into meadows and covers of illusion. . . . The sole criterion for me is whether it can sweep me with it into emotion or illusion of beauty, terror, tranquility, or even disgust" (30).

As the temptations of the emotions acquire greater force, the history turns more comic, more anxious, and more political. The physiological forms of affective criticism range from "excited puffs," "goose-flesh experience," and spinal shivers to the gut-wrenching, but Wimsatt and Beardsley also comment on "the hallucinative power of drama," demonstrating how forceful can be the effect of emotions in troubled political times (30). The willing suspension of disbelief corrodes the skepticism about emotion necessary to maintain objectivity, and panic in the public results. When such hallucinatory effects occur in the theater, the consequences are minimal. But the ease with which emotions take over the public is also an indicator of political turmoil. Wimsatt and Beardsley, for example, take great delight in giving the example of Stefan Schnabel, noted player of Nazi roles in radio dramas during World War II: Schnabel received numerous letters of complaint from the public, and one lady in particular wrote to say that she had reported him to General MacArthur. But we should remember how emotionally powerful was the image of the Nazis and remind ourselves that image-makers of the period were not exactly innocent of encouraging an exaggerated picture of them. We should remember as well that Schnabel was an actor in Orson Welles's radio hoax of 1938, during which an anxious population, watching Germany on the eve of World War II, believed that Martians had invaded.

The important point to stress is that aesthetic effects, whether of emotion or beauty, act in the words of Edmund Burke, which Wimsatt and Beardsley cite, "by relaxing the solids of the whole system" (30). During the early years of the cold war the system was everything. The world hovered on the brink of chaos, and the Allies tried to impose an ordered sharing of power and to establish precise national borders. People were mindful of how easily a previous generation had been taken over by their emotions and anxieties, of how strongly they had first demanded charismatic leaders, and of how swiftly they had then relinquished control to them and succumbed to hatred and violence.

A population of readers desirous of being swept away by emotions of terror and disgust must have been frightening for the objective critics in Wimsatt and Beardsley. The emotions of the day certainly made a difficult balancing act for politicians, as Douglas MacArthur and Henry Wallace, to note polar opposites, were to discover. Such emotions were to prove no less difficult for literary critics and writers of every political stripe, as the 1949 dispute over awarding the Bollingen Prize to Ezra Pound and recent debates about T. S. Eliot's apparent anti-Semitism and about the racist tendencies of the Southern Agrarians vividly illustrate.[9] The New Critics in general and Wimsatt in particular have become in recent years symbols of authoritarianism in criticism and of absolute conviction in politics, as we continue to replay issues and emotions associated with the cold war.[10] Indeed, the critical tendency today to condemn the New Critics as ethically or politically repressive because of their desire to control emotions or to attain objectivity is ruled by the same equation between emotion and

[9] See, for example, Christopher Ricks, *T. S. Eliot and Prejudice* (Boston: Faber, 1985).

[10] Attacks in this vein on the New Critics and on Wimsatt in particular are numerous, but since I intend to turn to the writings of Stephen Greenblatt I will note his criticism of Wimsatt's authoritarian and totalizing disposition. See Greenblatt, *Shakespearean Negotiations*, 3, 165n.1, and *Learning to Curse*, 1–2.

morality that has proved so unstable in the political world of the postwar era. Small wonder that Wimsatt and Beardsley attempt to replace emotion as the standard of literary judgment with objective principles. Their demand that we read carefully expresses the belief that we can gain some measure of control over conflict in interpretation, and it foreshadows later preoccupations in both criticism and politics with the languages of propaganda and ideology. Emotional disputes about ideology and misleading language are hardly new. They reflect in their form and vocabulary the conflicts of the cold war era.

The objective critic as defined by Wimsatt and Beardsley hopes to temper human emotions, whether the author's or the reader's, by locating them in the poetic object, where the affective connections between cause and effect may be scrutinized with disinterest and reason. That the analogy between politics and the republic of the poem has worked for so many years, and remains today in many forms, demonstrates its power and perhaps our need for it. Poetry in this view offers a vision of a less violent world, although one may question whether it has anything to do with the real one. But objective criticism does make a genuine contribution. It embraces as its principal goal the need to understand "how poetry makes ideas thick and complicated enough to hold on to emotions" (35). Its plea that we consider poetry as a discourse about emotions and objects, that we contemplate it as a pattern of knowledge, and that we try to recover what is reliable about the structure of emotive objects reads today as an attempt to take the first steps toward an understanding of how emotions are induced in us by different uses of language. This goal allows the willing student of poetry to recover the structure of emotive objects, to test their verity, and to acknowledge the quality of the feelings aroused by them, despite the "waning of human culture" (39). "In short," Wimsatt and Beardsley write, "though cultures have changed and will change, poems remain and explain" (39).

Objective criticism is a method designed for a chaotic and dangerous time, for a period that believes in the waning of human culture and finds solace in epistemological skepticism and relativism. It strives to prevent our hearts from running away with our heads and with emotions in excess of the facts by positing an objective basis for meaning, one in which our emotions could be monitored, verified, and held in check. "Art is a *cold* sphere," Wimsatt and Beardsley conclude, following Thomas Mann's formulation (31). In the cold sphere of art, we need to be aware of the facts and to be wary of emotions in excess of the facts. It turns out that Wimsatt and Beardsley were worried about another cold sphere as well.

The Critic Who Refused to Come in from the Cold

In a 1976 essay, later included in *Criticism in the Wilderness* (1980), Geoffrey Hartman wrote about certain rumors unsettling the university. "Rumors abound," Hartman announced, "that the New Criticism, no longer fighting for its place in the university but accepted as the standard of an urbane and teachable discipline, is being challenged by a still newer criticism" (226). It seems that this newer criticism, deconstruction, has been with us for much longer than Hartman's history would allow. But he is accurate in his assessment. The conference that introduced continental ideas to the United States took place at Johns Hopkins University in 1966, but its proceedings were not published until 1970, and it took until at least 1976 for deconstruction to gain a strong foothold. The New Criticism had been gently rocked over the years by existentialism and phenomenology, but in 1970 it still remained secure in its cradle, although not for long. What came "after the New Criticism," as Frank Lentricchia explained in his 1980 title, was the deconstructive criticism of the Yale school—Jacques Derrida, Harold Bloom, J. Hillis Miller, Paul de Man, and Geoffrey Hartman—which means that the New Criticism had held sway as an institutional force for more than thirty years.

It is by now an old story or at least a familiar one that the New Critics and the newer Yale critics do not really differ as much as one would expect in their views of literature. We assume that politics is another matter. But the newer criticism is as much a cold war criticism as the New Criticism was. I will not pursue directly a comparison between the poetics of the New Criticism and American deconstruction, although I will imply that similarities exist. More important to my argument will be to provide a sense of how deconstruction in its

American form relates to cold war politics. For this reason, Hartman is a good choice as an object of study because he is most concerned among the Yale critics with mediating between the United States and the Continent, and he may also have the strongest emotional ties to events of World War II, as his recent and welcomed turn to Holocaust studies reveals. If I were interested in a less conflicted or a more individual version of American deconstruction, J. Hillis Miller or Harold Bloom would be important, for Miller has been a powerful force in the institutionalization of deconstruction, and Bloom, although he has now broken with the Yale school, was its most idiosyncratic member. In the criticism of Hartman we find the desire to resolve conflict without either taming or identifying with it, and consequently the conflict of interpretations has an urgent and quite political quality in his writings.

This quality first exposes itself in Hartman's embrace of what he calls heterogeneous critics and texts. In his remarks on Kenneth Burke, one of our most heterogeneous thinkers, Hartman reveals his central concern as a critic during the 1970s:

> Books are always battles, mental war, but are they acceptable substitutes for conflict? Burke's motto for *The Grammar of Motives*, "ad bellum purificandum" ("to purify warfare"), leaves it unclear whether war can be removed, or only cleansed of darker ends. The analysis of what "war" means, why it is a permanent feature of human existence (the war to end all wars having proved to be, by 1939, just another war) is conducted by Burke in terms that are anthropological and theological rather than narrowly political. (93)

Burke's 1945 *Grammar of Motives* proposes as its goal to replace the conflict created by international situations with the quandaries of symbolic action. To replace the open conflict of international situations with symbolic action or to cleanse war of darker ends is as good a description of the cold war effect as any that we might desire. To be narrowly political is judged too dangerous by cold warriors, so they enlarge political conflict to include economic policies, trade issues, propaganda, and technological competition.

Hartman shares Burke's desire to conduct criticism in symbolic rather than narrowly political terms, but like Burke he has a hard time not commenting on politics. Hartman's turn toward anthropology and theology appears retrograde (and he has been criticized for it by Edward Said and others). It seems hopelessly out of step with those continental critics who proclaim the death of anthropology and the ideological corruption of religion. Nevertheless, Hartman shares with Burke and the New Critics an insight that more dogmatic poststructuralists fail to grasp: religious rhetoric and charismatic attractions are always essential components of both literature and politics.

If Burke failed in his theory of symbolic action—and I believe that he did—it was because he was ultimately more interested in political action than in symbolism as it has been traditionally defined, that is, as a means of achieving disinterested contemplation. The same may be said about Hartman. On the one hand, he appears to view literature as an aesthetic phenomenon distinct from or opposed to society. He calls art "a radical critique of representation," a phrase that makes little sense if we view "representation" as exclusively aesthetic rather than social, for Hartman is interested, after all, in the anthropological and theological (115). Society is for him "anti-art" since, "at best, it channels creativity into the minor arts of 'design' (decoration, fashion, posters, textiles, pottery) and, at worst, lures it into the pseudoworld of the communications media: advertising, propaganda, entertainment, journalism" (183). In such judgments, we find the motivation behind Hartman's requirement, à la Matthew Arnold, that the critic accept the wilderness as the promised land and abandon the hope of becoming a *terrae filius*. If society is so corrupt and violent, it is better to stay in the wilderness: *"Périssons en résistant,"* Hartman seems to cry, with Arnold, echoing the words of Obermann.

On the other hand, Hartman's aestheticism and intellectual elitism constantly betray themselves as tactics to resist what Wimsatt would have called the "waning of culture." Would that literature were distinct from propaganda and ideology, would that society were really antiart, he seems to say. For then we would be presented with a new path leading away from the anxieties, violence, and corruption of the political world. Hartman makes a titanic effort to describe literature as this new path. He offers descriptions of literature as the domain in which totalitarian and authoritarian principles have been vanquished.

He presents literary works and their reading as a democratic sphere in which we find a private and free mode of expression:

> Each work of art, and each work of reading, is potentially a demonstration of freedom: of the capacity we have for making sense by a mode of expression that is our own, despite political, religious, or psychological interference. Because of the modern attitude that politics is fate, Malraux called art an "antifate"; and there is, at present, an adversary relation between civilized discourse and the political and technological drive for security—through thought-control or the subordination of the arts (and even the universities) to specified practical ends. (2)

Nevertheless, the freedom of literature is hopelessly tainted as Hartman describes it. The symbolism of disinterestedness, art's peaceful autonomy, keeps breaking down because it is designed so obviously as an antidote to society's ills and because it is so easily contaminated by them, and skepticism and negativity eventually take over. Literature does not provide the freedom to be someone, somewhere, or a certain way. It presents the freedom to be reactionary and to define oneself as other, uncommon, strange, or uncanny. The principle of freedom in literary work and reading relies on the "willingness to receive figurative language" (27), the respect of "heterogeneity" (26), and "the power of negative thinking" (31). The literary critic is, as a result, "deliberately hesitant" and "affected by a kind of stutter" (32).

American deconstruction as practiced by Hartman prefers fragmentation to wholeness, thereby avoiding the dreaded desire for totality throbbing at the heart of totalitarian movements. Deconstruction sits instead in a kingdom of ruins where it embraces the vanquished of history. Critics arm themselves against the dictator within by refusing to dictate anything; deconstruction proposes a type of analysis, "a hermeneutics of indeterminacy," that has "renounced the ambition to master or to demystify its subject (text, psyche) by technocratic, predictive, or authoritarian formulas" (41). It is designed to avoid giving away the critical spirit to political movements. "This criticism without a name," as Hartman sums it up, "cannot be called a movement. It is too widespread, miscellaneous, and without a program. Its only program is a revaluation of criticism itself . . ." (41).

Hartman's attempt to establish literature as an instrument of symbolic action for democracy produces a view of criticism that is hobbled by its own obsession with totalitarian influences. In short, his view of criticism strongly reflects the politics of the cold war era, in which anxieties about violence and betrayal taint the very idea of the political. The republic of criticism imagined by Hartman does not escape this effect. Indeed, internal conflicts threaten to destroy the critical spirit itself, and the metaphors by which critics define their enterprise begin to mirror the chaos of the world, often anticipating the terrible consequences promised by cold war hostilities: the world burst into flame, hammered into fragments, broken into ruins, left to none but the vanquished.

In the mid to late 1970s we saw the cold war emerge with renewed force after a short period of détente, and the metaphors embraced by the criticism of the decade reflect this change. The Carter presidency defended human rights but neglected détente, introducing a new era of uncertainty in cold war relations. In February 1977 Brezhnev called Carter's championing of human rights a pseudohumanitarian gesture and denounced his correspondence with the dissident Sakharov. Brezhnev then refused to meet with his American counterpart until after the signing of the Salt II Treaty. Meanwhile, Carter supported weapon plans favored by conservatives: the cruise missile, the Minuteman III, and the Trident submarine; and the Soviets and Americans took opposite sides in Africa in the conflict between Ethiopia and Somalia. The Salt II Treaty was signed in June 1979, after a long delay, but it went unratified by the Senate when the Soviets invaded Afghanistan in December 1979. By January 1980 the president had promulgated the Carter Doctrine, defining any attempt to gain control of the Persian Gulf by outside forces as a direct assault on the vital interests of the United States, and he had announced that we would not send athletes to the 1980 Summer Olympics in Moscow. In four years the cold war had turned from détente to crisis.

It is remarkable that literary theorists embraced critical hesitancy, "the hermeneutics of indeterminacy," to use Hartman's phrase, at the very moment when Carter's stuttering diplomacy entered cold war politics. The metaphors used by Hartman and others to describe deconstructive criticism invoke this historical context (the scandal of Nixon, the transitional period of Ford, and the hesitancy of Carter) as well as summon a series of images associated with the emotionally charged climate of the cold war period. Hartman's call for a history of the vanquished seems in particular to be a product of the Carter era. Such metaphors and images cannot be ignored, but neither can they carry by themselves the full burden of a political analysis. Hartman's more overt political statements make it clear, however, that these metaphors have not seeped willy-nilly into critical discourse but are coherent expressions of reigning political sensibilities. They are the figurative embodiments of the popular opinions and the political wisdom of the day.

Nowhere is this tendency more apparent than in Hartman's embrace of American deconstruction's requirement that criticism turn upon itself. Hartman, we saw, resists the idea that criticism might be systematic. In fact, he begins *Criticism in the Wilderness* with the assertion that it is a "book of experiences rather than a systematic defense of literary studies" (1). Deconstruction, according to Hartman, refuses to be named; it desires no connection with the solidarity of a movement. It will not have its program marked by the ambition of a capital letter (deconstruction, never Deconstruction, often "deconstruction," or the "so-called deconstruction," as Hillis Miller likes to write).[11] Rather, its program, if it can be said to possess one, is only to criticize itself.

At some points this attitude appears to be the comic complement to Carter's confession that he had committed adultery many times in his heart. It certainly reflects the dominant political advice of the late 1970s that Americans should monitor more closely their political process, their dependence on oil, and their commitment to human rights and the poor. Hartman does not refer openly to any of these trends. He has in mind, I believe, an earlier development in the history of politics, which had only recently reemerged in depleted form. I am referring to

[11] Am I going too far when I see a manifestation of this fear of the capital letter in the widespread confusion over how to enter "Paul de Man" in indexes and bibliographies? The current practice is to leave the "d" in the lower case even when it starts the entry. Another is to treat de Man like nobility, listing him as "Man, Paul de." How strange is this concurrent refusal of the capital letter and embrace of nobility!

politics driven by charismatic leadership. Nixon was never a charismatic leader (as Kennedy had been), although he was elected by a landslide, but the opinion of many by the mid 1970s was that Nixon bore some resemblance to an earlier, more evil political leadership that had used charismatic means to mislead people and to seize power. Hartman's attempt to reorient criticism toward self-reflexivity is, like Carter's many calls for Americans to look within, dominated by a fear of such charismatic power. It expresses the suspicion that we have become the enemy, that consciousness is the enemy, and it seeks a remedy by turning consciousness against itself.

Hartman's word for this entire dilemma is in fact "charisma." In more general terms, he follows Burke and Walter Benjamin, arguing that theology has become both the "secret passion within modern politics" and the source of its menace (82). In a long reading of Benjamin, in which the emblem of society is the machine-theater, Hartman traces the modernization of theology and the aestheticization of politics to "the old cultic desire for control of self and others" (83).[12] "Our fascination with technique," Hartman urges, "with neat solutions and totalitarian harmonies, inflicts on the psyche and body of man a new, quasi-religious shame that turns them into hunchbacks, unless they are coordinated and programmed like the machine" (83). The result is the double bind defined as charisma. We desire personal power and freedom; this is the driving force in democracy. But we fear the excessive personal power and freedom—the will to power—of totalitarian and charismatic leaders. As Hartman expresses it, "we fear the restoration of wonder as much as its loss: the danger of being suckered by charismatic persons and their miracles of rare device" (83).

Hartman's solution to the problem, as far as there is one in the modern age of totalitarian desire, resides in the literary work, whose "radical" nature opposes strangeness, hesitancy, and stuttering to the monolith of charismatic power. And yet we have already seen that literature in Hartman's view also holds a charismatic force. Consequently, Hartman again finds himself following Burke in the realization that politics sometimes uses aesthetic and religious power to serve

[12] Hartman here foreshadows the criticism of Stephen Greenblatt, who, it is no accident, was also influenced by Benjamin.

ideological deception. Burke had found in *Mein Kampf* a bastardization of fundamentally religious patterns of thought, and he noted repeatedly the evocative power of Hitler's metaphors.[13] Hartman extends this analysis to Nietzsche, whose will to power was both a religious and an aesthetic ideal that contributed to the philosophy of totalitarianism, and to Adorno's and Horkheimer's view that totalitarianism would have been impossible without the Enlightenment "belief" in Reason and its consequent purging of nonrational and nonbureaucratic ideas. As Wimsatt had argued before him, Hartman sees a danger in the willing suspension of disbelief, and he recommends a healthy dose of skepticism and negative thinking about art. "What we appreciate as exemplary in art," he explains, "we admire and fear as 'charismatic' in public life. If it is hard enough to tell charlatan from genius in art, it often seems impossible to distinguish between creative and destructive portions of the spirit in a significant politician or religious leader" (99).

There is, however, only one way to avoid charismatic leadership. We must learn how to read, Hartman argues, how to scrutinize literature and representational forms in a way that reveals their complexity and heterogeneity. The key to defeating charisma is to understand its paradoxes. In short, the antidote to charismatic power is to focus on its weaknesses and self-contradictions. We derive the power to resist charisma by discovering those areas where charisma has undone itself. But this means that we continue to be fascinated by the spell of the charismatic figure, even if it leads to its apparent undoing. Whence the argument for the self-deconstructive text, which is not ascribed to the abilities, conscience, or intellect of an author—for this would again be to fall into a dangerous bardolatry—but to the nature of textuality itself. "Language power," as it is so awkwardly called during this period, is embraced as the polar opposite of human power or charisma. By embracing the radical power of language to deconstruct itself, we supposedly gain a model for avoiding the dangers of charismatic leadership as well as a new ideal of moral character. It is worth noting, however, that those figures most often associated with self-

[13] Kenneth Burke, "The Rhetoric of Hitler's 'Battle,'" *The Philosophy of Literary Form* (Berkeley and Los Angeles: University of California Press, 1973 [1941]), 191–220.

deconstructive textuality—Freud, Marx, Nietzsche, Saussure, Rousseau, Hölderlin, Shelley, Keats, Emerson, and Melville, to name the usual cast of characters—are hardly presented as meek exemplars of self-effacement but are themselves subject to the most exaggerated forms of hero worship.

Even if we avoid this kind of hero worship by resolutely clinging to the theory that language is responsible in itself for self-reflexivity, we cannot escape the tendency to cast language in the mold of a new charismatic leader, who either imprisons us in its house or frees us on a whim. Hartman succumbs to this temptation many times, although less completely than de Man and Hillis Miller. At the end of his long analysis of charisma, Hartman criticizes de Man's belief that *"language* rather than politics is fate" (108). Instead, he argues that power is associated with spirit, and that language, like Ariel, is "the free servant of an *unknown* power" (108). But Hartman knows no other way to define this *"unknown"* except by reference to language. Charismatic power reemerges in the linguistic operation of capitalization, in which any word, the word *Word* itself, becomes a source of sublime power when marked by the capital letter: "Capitalize or foreground any word, the word *Word* itself, and you recreate a sublime or allegorical form: a quasitheological, hypostatized entity" (114).

Toward the end of the book Hartman provides what is perhaps the clearest expression of this dilemma. Here also he makes contact most explicitly with the politics of the cold war era. In the self-reflexivity of the text, he locates a new humanism, which does not spiritualize itself as a charismatic force but attempts to make us aware of the material culture in which human beings live. The answer to unlocking this knowledge is to adopt a form of "thick description," à la Clifford Geertz, in short, to recognize the infinite variety, heterogeneity, and uncanniness of language. It is also to embrace a criticism that can teach us the nature of authority and the difference between a truly ethical politics and others, whether democratic or totalitarian, that bend human beings to their unjust authority:

> What authority do texts enjoy? Why do we continue to rely on
> them? . . . The oldest detective story keeps being reenacted.
> On every side there is a self-incriminating lust for evidence. . . .

Evidence fails or is disabled, and the unusual or ungovernable types of interpretation come into play. Science fiction too creates worlds in which the forces are unknown, and all appearances and testimonies risk being false. . . . Yet the perplexity that art arouses in careful readers and viewers is hardly licentious. . . . It recalls the prevalence of propaganda, both in open societies that depend on conversation, jawboning, advertising, bargaining, and in controlled societies that can become sinister and inquisitional, adding to their torture chamber the subtlest brainwashing and conditioning devices without giving up the brazen and reiterated lie. Can hermeneutics of indeterminacy, any irony however deeply practiced and nurtured by aesthetic experience, withstand either society while they are still distinguishable? (283)

Criticism truly finds the promised land in the wilderness if the above description captures accurately the reality of the civilized world. Better to discover a new society, an antisociety, in the world of language, to recoil from the evil representations of both democracy and totalitarianism, if indeed they can be distinguished, and to discover a new freedom and a new conscience in our own perplexity. If coming in from the cold means having to live in such societies, if it means accelerating an alliance between them, it is better for the critic to remain in the cold. Such, as least, seems to be the dominant sentiment at work in deconstruction's suspicion of society and embrace of the emotionless, inhumane, and abstract sphere of language power.

Deconstruction in America grew up during the Carter years, when charisma was nowhere in sight but greatly feared. It expressed the cold war mentality through the medium of language power, and it placed in a criticism preoccupied with language the hope of coming to an understanding of that power. But times were changing fast. Charisma would soon assume center stage once more with the election of Ronald Reagan, and a new metaphor, economics, would emerge to complicate the poststructuralist ideal of language. Hartman foresees some of these changes. He calls for "thick description," predicting the emphasis on cultural criticism important in the 1980s, and when he worries that literary criticism will succumb to fiscal retrenchment he foresees the fate of the arts in the age of economic metaphors. Finally, his fear that Ph.D.'s in history or English will abandon liberal education for law school and his complaint that first-year M.B.A.'s make more money than the average university professor reverberate with the tremors of the coming Reagan revolution (295).

Shakespeare and Company

Also appearing in 1980, along with Hartman's *Criticism in the Wilderness,* was Stephen Greenblatt's *Renaissance Self-Fashioning,* a book that takes seriously the anthropology of Geertz and the desire of the self to be independent and free. Greenblatt proposes a reading of Renaissance authors in which building a powerful self is an important, if morally dubious, enterprise. The book marks the strange transition between Carter's anxious and self-conscious humanitarianism and the unreflective bravado of Reagan's economic policies, which were designed "to make America strong again." In one amazing year the cold war would find a different course, moving from Carter's plea that Americans do without and make sacrifices for the world to Reagan's declaration of the good-time years. In 1980 Reagan set the cold war on an economic course, determined to bankrupt the Soviet Union, and Americans came to believe, to recall Herb Cohen's book of the same year, that "you can negotiate anything." By 1988 Greenblatt would close the Reagan era with another book in which he shifts from the metaphors of Geertz's and Carter's "anthropology" to the economic language of the Reagan presidency. In *Shakespearean Negotiations* Greenblatt surpasses even Herb Cohen's optimistic advice to business-men to use the Shakespearean theater as a new model for the ideal cold war polity, this time basing the democratic ideal on the freewheeling negotiations of the marketplace. The richness and the complexity of Greenblatt's project reveal themselves in his seemingly endless ability to mediate between the humanitarianism of the Carter years and the laissez-faire philanthropy of Reaganomics, as well as to bear the contradiction between the aesthetic vocabulary of "improvisation," used in the 1980 *Renaissance Self-Fashioning,* and the economic language of "negotiation," used in the 1988 book on Shakespeare.

The conclusion of *Renaissance Self-Fashioning,* the book that launched Greenblatt and the new historicism, recounts a personal anecdote familiar in the political climate of the Carter era. Greenblatt finds himself aboard a plane—then the zone of conflict in which cold war terrorism was being played out—traveling from Baltimore to Boston, in other words, from the site of the "structuralist controversy" to the American city chosen by his immigrant ancestors. He wants to reread Geertz's *Interpretation of Cultures,* but another passenger imposes upon him in a strange fashion. The somber man sitting next to him is on the way to visit his ailing son who has lost the will to live and the ability to speak. Stung with the horror of his task and resolved to restore his son's desire to live, the terrified father asks Greenblatt to do him a favor: he asks Greenblatt to help him practice reading lips so that he may communicate with his dying son. "Would you say, soundlessly," the man requests, "'I want to die. I want to die'" (255).

But Greenblatt refuses to fulfill the request. It is not for a want of altruism but because of fear. Greenblatt confesses that he is frightened that the sentence, once spoken, will act as an incantation and bring his life to an end. Perhaps, more important, considering that the scene takes place on a plane, he is afraid of terrorism: "I could not do what the man had asked in part because I was afraid that he was, quite simply, a maniac and that once I had expressed the will to die, he would draw a hidden knife and stab me to death or, alternatively, activate some device secreted on board the plane that would blow us all to pieces . . ." (256). Greenblatt punctuates the anecdote by relating it to the thesis of his book. The anecdote brings home to him his own resemblance to those Renaissance figures who understand "that in our culture to abandon self-fashioning is to abandon the craving for freedom, and to let go of one's stubborn hold upon selfhood, even selfhood conceived as a fiction, is to die" (257). The critic's own inability to help the distraught father bears witness to a similar need to sustain the illusion that he is the principal maker of his own identity.

Of course, the anecdote resonates on a political level as well. Greenblatt lives in a world in which hostages are taken, terrorists strike out, maniacs roam, and the powerful seem incapable of doing anything about it. Hidden weapons menace his world, and the notion that an explosive device is "secreted" somewhere on the plane, although passed off by Greenblatt as California paranoia, reminds one more of

the general terrors derived from living in cold war times. When Reagan
came to power, he promised to allay these fears, to make Americans
strong again, and to prove that the powerful would not be victims
anymore. He would accomplish this feat in the same way that he had
himself come to greatness. He would teach Americans how to act. He
would show them by the strength of his charisma how to be proud,
powerful, and generous. He would teach values to remake his age. He
would instruct Americans how to refashion themselves in his likeness
and to accept the belief that they could be free, independent, strong,
and fearless.

By 1988 Greenblatt had lost his fear of flying, and he is no longer
terrified of the dead. *Shakespearean Negotiations* opens by summon-
ing a series of mortuary riddles. Just as Hartman had argued that "our
life remains a feast of mortuary riddles and jokes that must be an-
swered" (301), Greenblatt finds in the voices of the dead his most
prized objects. Calling professors of literature "middleclass shamans,"
he confesses that he hears his own voice in the most intense moments
of communing with the dead. Like Anatole France, then, Greenblatt
speaks of his own age apropos of Shakespeare's. *Shakespearean Negotiations* proposes a theory of social energy to understand Shakespeare's theater, but given the historical context of the book, it remains
to be seen whether social energy is not a metaphor for the newfound
economic optimism of the Reagan years.[14]

Shakespearean Negotiations begins by telling a story. We used to
believe, thanks to the New Criticism, that works of literature are "pre-
cipitated out of a sublime confrontation between a total artist and a
totalizing society" (2). (Greenblatt cites Wimsatt in both *Shakespearean Negotiations* and *Learning to Curse* as a source of this view,
although one wonders how Greenblatt has managed to forget about

---

[14]Marlon Ross, in "Contingent Predilections: The Newest Historicism and the Question of Method, *Centennial Review* 34, no. 4 (1990): 485–538, makes a strong case for
the implicit connections between the new historicism and Reaganomics, noting that their
opposition becomes a true friendship because "we always subvert the ones we love"
(510). More important, he shows that the new historicism has become the method to
replace the New Criticism because it allows an instructor "to teach materials that can be
contained in and by the American classroom" (514).

"The Intentional Fallacy.") But now we have grown uneasy with "monolithic entities," he suggests, and we are looking for better ideas. Greenblatt explains that his uneasiness first led him to turn to the rubric of power, but it implies too much control, he discovers—more than the exercise of authority and force during the Renaissance commands—and he looks for another explanation. Greenblatt's itinerary as a theorist is the quest for a better method of analysis, one that can analyze power without giving it too much power. It is also a story about how to discuss the accomplishments, goals, and genius of great artists, without refashioning them into "total artists."

The theory of social energy apparently provides Greenblatt with the method necessary to accomplish his desire. The theory redescribes the workings of power in terms of an economic model that reveals that market forces dissipate forms of totalitarian power ("totalizing society," "total artists"). Social energy (*energia*) has a stunning organizational capacity without being top-heavy. Its power resides in many discrete units, and it is impossible for one person to seize power for very long. More significant, the theory of social energy holds that the circulation of energy is inherently unstable: it has no single source, and it surges in no particular direction. Rather, it is characterized by endless transaction. A method of reading that seeks to tap this energy will not believe in a "whole reading," Greenblatt notes. Nor will it seek to be systematic, totalizing, or totalitarian. The vision is "necessarily more fragmentary" (4). Nevertheless, the shift to the particular and the anecdotal offers definite gains for the critic. We come to view language as a collective creation, and we realize that works of literature, theater, and art address their audiences as a "collectivity." "The Shakespearean theater," above all, Greenblatt claims, "depends upon a felt community" (5).

The Shakespearean theater begins to emerge as a new model for community in the age of totalitarianism. It only needs to be better understood to recognize its virtues. The theater teaches the critic to see how boundaries are marked between cultural practices and social classes, to discover how representations generate pleasure and anxiety, and to understand the illusion of aesthetic autonomy. Remarkably, Greenblatt does not wish, as has been the custom in poststructuralism, to strip away and to discard "the enchanted impression of aesthetic autonomy" (5). Rather, he wants to understand its objective conditions, which means, in effect, that he intends to study the public dimension of aesthetic representation. The project is not unlike Wimsatt's, except that Greenblatt does not seem to despise the fact that entertainments organize emotion. Unlike Hartman, he appears to see in advertising a mode of social and aesthetic participation and not a degraded form of communication. Greenblatt does not locate the symbolism of ideal social organization in either the aesthetic artifact—the form of the poem, for example—or in the nature of language, but in an order of aesthetic participation that is the theater. Consequently, the transactions of theatrical pleasure become the sources of social reform, stability, politics, ethics, and democratic ideals. The theater is the realm of social energy as such, which Greenblatt defines in terms that strikingly recall the market economy as conceived by Reaganomics:

> In its aesthetic modes, social energy must have a minimal predictability—enough to make simple repetitions possible—and a minimal range: enough to reach out beyond a single creator or consumer to some community, however constricted. Occasionally, and we are generally interested in these occasions, the predictability and range will be far greater: large numbers of men and women of different social classes and divergent beliefs will be induced to explode with laughter or weep or experience a complex blend of anxiety and exaltation. . . .
>   If one longs, as I do, to reconstruct these negotiations, one dreams of finding an originary moment. . . . But the quest is fruitless, for there is no originary moment, no pure act of untrammeled creation. In place of a blazing genesis, one begins to glimpse something that seems at first far less spectacular: a subtle, elusive set of exchanges, a network of trades and trade-offs, a jostling of competing representations, a negotiation between joint-stock companies. Gradually, these complex, ceaseless borrowings and lendings have come to seem to me more important, more poignant even, than the epiphany for which I had hoped. (6–7)[15]

---

[15] I add another description of the same genre: "Plays are made up of multiple exchanges, and the exchanges are multiplied over time, since to the transactions through which the work first acquired social energy are added supplementary transactions through which the work renews its power in changed circumstances" (20).

Greenblatt's prose runs the gamut of emotions, as one might expect of someone jostled by a throng of traders and negotiators. It is the story of a conversion to an economic point of view. As the cold war comes to its close, Greenblatt, after much resistance, finds endless exchanges and negotiations "poignant" and, I might add, politically sound. The theater presents one with a society in which convictions and class do not divide people, for social energy cuts across differences and "trickles down" from the high and mighty to the low and abject, inducing all to explode together in laughter, anxiety, and exaltation. The theater itself is created by moving stories from one cultural zone to another. The stories and signifiers are themselves untouched by the transactions (like money), as they are appropriated again and again by subjects whose negotiations blend to form a complex and unified community—or "communitas," which Victor Turner defines as a union based on the momentary breaking of the hierarchy that normally governs a community. Greenblatt actually ends the first chapter of *Shakespearean Negotiations* by enumerating the kinds of appropriations important to theatrical economy.[16] In short, the chain of exchanges found in the theater realizes both the ideal model of community and of history. It shows moments of hierarchy, authoritarianism, and totalizing power to be temporary effects in a heterogeneous and episodic ecosystem whose very nature will prevent such effects from gaining the upper hand and ensure the free and equal distribution of energy among all of its participants. Especially significant, the communitas of the theater excludes relatively little, for

[16] One of these appropriations seems to be the equivalent of the junk bond: "*Acquisition through Synecdoche or Metonymy.* Here the theater acquires cultural energy by isolating and performing one part or attribute of a practice that stands for the whole (often a whole that cannot be represented). For example, as I argue in chapter 3, verbal chafing becomes in Shakespeare's comedies not only a sign but a vital instance of an encompassing erotic heat otherwise impossible to stage in the public theater" (11). Another description stresses the importance of mergers: "individuals are themselves the products of collective exchange. In the Renaissance theater this collective nature is intensified by the artists' own participation in versions of joint-stock companies. In such companies individual ventures have their own sharply defined identities and interests (and their own initial capital), but to succeed they pool their resources, and they own essential properties in common" (12).

> the language of theater was astonishingly open: the most solemn
> formulas of the church and state could find their way onto the stage
> and mingle with the language of the marketplace. . . . For the circu-
> lation of social energy by and through the stage was not part of a
> single coherent, totalizing system. Rather it was partial, fragmentary,
> conflictual; elements were crossed, torn apart, recombined, set
> against each other; particular social parties were magnified by the
> stage, others diminished, exalted, evacuated. What then is the social
> energy being circulated? Power, charisma, sexual excitement, collec-
> tive dreams, wonder, desire, anxiety, religious awe, free-floating in-
> tensities of experience: in a sense the question is absurd, for every-
> thing produced by the society can circulate unless it is deliberately
> excluded from circulation. Under such circumstances, there can be no
> single method, no overall picture, no exhaustive and definitive cul-
> tural poetics. (19)

Greenblatt has been attacked for creating a picture of society in
which change and reform are impossible.[17] I think that this criticism
misses the point because it fails to recognize that Greenblatt's theater
of society constantly changes and reforms itself according to an economic law that regulates both morality and politics to the good. In
sum, if social reform, as we usually define it, is impossible, it does not
matter because it is unnecessary. Greenblatt's theater, like Reagan's
vision of America, attempts to take government off the backs of the
people. It deregulates the system as it has existed, claiming that rules
are unnecessary because the economy of the system has its own laws.
Social energy cannot belong to the powerful or to anyone else, so we
do not need government watchdogs and regulators. It is apparently in
the interest of everyone alike—the powerful and the weak, the businessman and the consumer, the rich and the poor—to make a good-
faith effort to participate in the network of trades and trade-offs. Here
Greenblatt describes the morality play of the market apropos of Shakespeare:

> Shakespeare the shareholder was presumably interested not simply in
> a good return on an individual play but in the health and success of
> his entire company as it related both to those who helped regulate it
> and to its audience. Each individual play may be said to make a small
> contribution to the general store of social energy possessed by the

[17] See Greenblatt's response in *Learning to Curse,* 164–66, 182n.3.

theater and hence to the sustained claim that the theater can make on
its real and potential audience. (14)

The Shakespearean theater levels power and distributes it equally to
all; it represents the perfect society, in which everyone gets a fair return
on a just investment, and democracy is regulated by innate principle.

One wonders whether these passages were written tongue in cheek.
It is clear that Greenblatt has little but contempt for Reagan and yet
seems to have adopted wholesale the major metaphors of his presidency.[18] If the vision of social energy is a private joke, a Shakespearean
parable ironizing the glory of the monarch, then those who would
make the comparison between Greenblatt and Reagan, myself included, are dupes. But why create such a drama in this day and age?
Reagan was not Greenblatt's patron, and elsewhere Greenblatt does
not spare the harshest words of scorn for the ex-actor. It does not seem
that a man of Greenblatt's intelligence could be unaware of the connections between his theories and Reagan's policies. The most satisfy-
ing explanation is to embrace the irony that Reaganomics and Greenblatt's own intellectual odyssey share similar goals. Greenblatt's theories take him from his early and uneasy embrace of the virtues of self-
fashioning to an attempt to find a way of describing the means by
which individuals fashion themselves through cultural and collective
representations. In short, he tries to mediate between the egotism of
the self and its attendant political horrors by designing a system that
naturally limits the power that individuals and systems can accumu-

---

[18] In "That's America," *London Review of Books* 10 (29 September 1988): 6 and 8,
Greenblatt makes his feelings about Reagan absolutely clear, claiming

> the state is merged with the President's body but the President's body becomes a
> media event, a Hollywood fantasy. Even Reagan's intestinal polyps were given
> elaborate media treatment, with the publication of the detailed results of the Presi-
> dential proctoscopy and television coverage (complete with animated diagrams) of
> his illness and recuperation from surgery. Vice-President Bush, always eager to
> emulate his hero, has released for publication the results of his most recent rectal
> examination, duly printed in the *New York Times*. The American public needs to
> be reassured that the country will be governed for another four years by a healthy
> asshole. (8)

It is also worth noting that Greenblatt makes a strong case for the relation between
Reagan's charisma and his cold war anticommunist stand.

late. Reaganomics likewise proposes to show that totalitarianism and big government are not economically viable. It claims that supply-side economics is not only compatible with democracy but the base on which it must be built. It preaches the fundamentally altruistic nature of the market.

A strong difference, however, does emerge between the new historicism and Reaganomics. Reagan is, of course, endlessly optimistic, whereas Greenblatt cannot sustain the optimism gained by his poignant embrace of the market. The theory of social energy, in effect, drops out of his book after the first chapter, making a curtain call only in the conclusion. The idea of charisma rules the remainder of the book, and charisma and social energy have little in common. Charisma in Greenblatt's reading does not encourage democratic ideals. It plays the same role found in Wimsatt and Hartman. It is the source, unlike social energy, of a false dependency on individual power and charm, and it produces the most despotic social organizations.

The *Henry IV* trilogy in Greenblatt's eyes reveals the horrors of charisma. It demonstrates that power originates in force and fraud even as it causes its victims to accept this power as legitimate. The trilogy makes it clear, then, that society has a large stake in individual power. Society desires charismatic leadership because it is in this embodiment of power that it sees its own achievements. "The ideal king," as Greenblatt puts it, "must be in large part the invention of the audience, the product of a will to conquer that is revealed to be identical to a need to submit" (63). But how does this view affect the theory of social energy? It suggests that the free circulation of social energy is ultimately unsatisfying because people in the system only grasp the existence of energy when it is manifested in the charismatic figure. People's own desires remain unreadable to them until they see desire personified in the leader.

Greenblatt views *1 Henry IV* as a commentary on a world in which theatricality guarantees charismatic leadership and state power. For theatricality allows charismatic leadership to emerge and people's desire to be read. The subsequent plays in the trilogy show this to be a horrible state of affairs. But it is not horrible because it shows people harmed by corruption and state power; the horror resides in the fact that power always works in this way, and therefore no matter how world weary we are, there is little to chose as an alternative, since any alternative is part of the same illusion of power. Indeed, according to Greenblatt, Shakespeare's trilogy shows that charisma creates its power by subverting itself (and I add that his interpretations of the comedies, tragedies, and romances rely on similar paradoxes concerning transgression, religious power, and anxieties about plenitude).

If this is the case, how does one deal with charisma? It cannot be attacked because attacks only give it a stronger hold over us. In the example of social energy, its circulation ensured a fair and just economy. It was in the tendency of transaction to lead to further transaction that Greenblatt located the democratic principle itself, for the theater did not permit the hypostasis necessary to totalitarian power. Instead, it encouraged the free circulation of energy. But charisma operates in an entirely different way. It is social energy turned nightmarish because each undoing of power ends by producing greater stability and more hypostasis. Power moves unchecked from source to destination, and the source and destination are the same entity.

It is in Greenblatt's reading of Shakespeare's trilogy, then, that the failings of the theory of social energy grow clear. For try as he might he cannot really distinguish between social energy and charisma.[19] This difficulty is particularly instructive for the Reagan years. During the age of Reagan social energy was tied to charisma. Reaganomics cut social programs, shifting responsibility from the government to the private sector. It became everyone's personal responsibility to look after the poor and to support the arts. But this tactic depended on the strength of Reagan's charisma. Since private philanthropy was not required by any form of government regulation, it could only be stimulated through the power of suggestion. Reagan hoped that people would turn philanthropic merely because he requested it. The entire model of laissez-faire philanthropy relied on the prestige and charisma of the president.

The *Henry IV* plays are the perfect dramas for the Reagan era,

[19] Perhaps not coincidentally, Wimsatt discusses *enargia*, which overlaps with *energia*, in the section of "The Affective Fallacy" devoted to the Grand Style and to the charismatic leadership of contagious teachers, poetic radiators, and magnetic rhapsodes (29–31).

and Greenblatt transforms them into allegories of the period. "The play," Greenblatt says of *1 Henry IV,* "awakens a dream of superabundance, which is given irresistible embodiment in Falstaff" (41). The comparison between Hal and Reagan is especially irresistible. Reagan was, of course, the Teflon president. He continued to hold power, despite the fact that he was accused of delegating too much power and of sleeping during cabinet meetings. In fact, he seemed to acquire power by displaying incompetence.[20] The more vulnerable he seemed, the more popular he became. Similarly, in Greenblatt's description, Hal emerges as a kind of juggler, especially in matters of the budget. He is "the prince and principle of falsification," who betrays this dream of abundance by "a continuous draining of the plenitude" (42). And yet it is not clear that Hal's conniving is proof of hypocrisy, for he appears to be mostly sincere. This is, after all, part of his charm. His "moral authority rests upon a hypocrisy so deep that the hypocrites themselves believe it" (55). Here is a different Shakespearean device— the play outside the play—and it reveals the presence of the play on the stage of world politics and the power of aesthetics to organize the social domain. It is no accident, if we accept Greenblatt's allegory, that Kenneth Branagh's "action-packed" version of *Henry V* made its way to the silver screen in 1990. Eight years of the Reagan presidency prepared the audience for this celebration of charisma, personal ambition, conquest, and national pride.

Greenblatt is unsure whether his reading of charisma can be attributed to Shakespeare or whether it is merely an effect of experiencing the plays over time. The questioning of power in the trilogy, so apparent to a modern audience, he argues, may have been invisible in Shakespeare's day: modern readers are "free to locate and pay homage to the play's doubts only because they no longer threaten us" (65). In short, skepticism about politics makes politics more dubious. Remarkably, Greenblatt asks how Shakespeare's skepticism would play in an even more cynical age, an age perhaps like our own, in which the desire for political survival depends on the sacrifice of political convictions: "Perhaps we should imagine Shakespeare writing at a moment when none

[20] As Greenblatt says of Reagan in "That's America," "the final triumph of the cult of personality is that it can expose its emptiness without losing its magic" (6).

of the alternatives for a resounding political commitment seemed satis-
factory; when the pressure to declare himself unequivocally an adher-
ent of one or another political faction seemed narrow, ethically coarse,
politically stupid; when the most attractive political solution seemed to
be to keep options open and the situation fluid." (175n.65). This is
suitable advice for our politics of the marketplace in which people
make wagers to stay in power and keep their options open rather than
holding to the power of their convictions. But it is questionable
whether we should wish it on Shakespeare.

Greenblatt's idea of the theater is a vision of liberal society gone
sour. He cannot convert to conservatism or accept on faith the idea
that the liberation of market forces will automatically save the unem-
ployed and the disenfranchised. Nor can he escape entirely the conservative belief in the inevitability of market forces. And so he exists in a
state of alienation, skepticism, and hesitancy, describing the conditions
of his own existence, sometimes with great scorn and other times with
great enthusiasm.[21] In his blacker moments Greenblatt claims that
"the founding of the modern state, like the self-fashioning of the modern prince, is shown to be based upon acts of calculation, intimidation,
and deceit. And these acts are performed in an entertainment for which
audiences, the subjects of this very state, pay money and applaud"
(51–52). In his moments of optimism he finds the market poignant and

---

[21] Describing his education at Yale University in *Learning to Curse,* Greenblatt reveals
that he is disposed to uncertainty. He directly opposes the character of W. K. Wimsatt—
a model of charisma itself in everything that Greenblatt writes—to his own:

> Wimsatt seemed to be eight feet tall and to be the possessor of a set of absolute
> convictions, but I was anything but certain. The best I could manage was a seminar
> paper that celebrated Sir Philip Sidney's narrative staging of his own confusions:
> "there is nothing so certain," Sidney wrote, "as our continual uncertainty." I
> briefly entertained a notion of going on to write a dissertation on uncertainty—to
> make a virtue of my own necessity—but the project seemed to me a capitulation, in
> thin disguise, to the hierophantic service to the mystery cult that I precisely wished
> to resist. For the radical uncertainty (what would now be called *aporia*) with which
> I was concerned was not, in the end, very different from the "mysterious and
> special status" of the concrete universal. (1)

Greenblatt's anecdotes about himself usually have the same message as those that he tells
about the Renaissance: they tend to resist totality and certainty by celebrating particularity and indeterminacy.

praises the morality of its transgressive power, its relentless desire to fight exclusion, and its ability to circulate power freely among its participants.

In a world in which belief has faded, the skeptical consciousness tries to turn its general disbelief toward a positive description of culture, a "poetics of culture," Greenblatt would call it. In place of totality, it tries to find the value of the fragment, whether it be in the form of the individual poem, language itself, or the chaotic circulation of the market economy. Greenblatt openly pursues this last alternative. He would replace the concept of the state, whether democratic or totalitarian, with the belief in a stateless state, the republic of the theater, in which "communitas" is achieved through the chaotic sharing of "power, charisma, sexual excitement, collective dreams, wonder, desire, anxiety, religious awe, free-floating intensities of experience" (19). No "total artist" and no "totalizing society" can have dominion in the republic of the theater. We are freed of the terrors of the modern dictator, the horrors of totalitarianism, and the burdensome responsibilities of democracy. Rather, the Shakespearean theater realizes the stuff that cold war dreams are made of: a totally free society produced by the revolution of totality against itself.

Criticism After the Cold War

The powerful differences between democracy and totalitarianism have had the effect of dispelling the hope that we could ever agree about what freedom for human beings is. We confront a philosophical equivalent of the Truman Doctrine, in which the world is divided into two radically divided camps, each loyal to a different conception of freedom. One defines freedom in terms of the ability to pursue desire, opportunity, and happiness; the other defines freedom as liberation from such desires. Each makes a devastating attack on the other, and by the end of the argument freedom no longer exists. It too has become part of the totality, and we are left with the vision of a monolith, in which everything is under control. "Reason," "truth," "law," "institution," "government," "politics," "morality"—these words have become our curse words because they symbolize the totality that we hate.

In the last four decades we have pursued models of judging that use no criteria because we are terrified of criteria.[22] We have abandoned standards for fear of being standardized. We have divinized individuality and scorned community because the cold warriors have told us that community is the harbinger of totalitarianism. Because we have been overtaken by a powerful anxiety about community, we have looked for every means possible to embrace disagreement and to prove it impossible to understand what could ever justify agreement, all the while remaining blind to the fact that this is the cold war effect par excellence.

The skepticism of cold war criticism has the same effect as the Truman Doctrine. It divides the world between antagonistic poles: the totalitarian and the democratic, the powerful and the powerless, the rich and the poor, the major and the minor. The irony remains, however, that these poles threaten to collapse at any moment. Inherent in the discourse of the powerless, poor, and minor, we must admit if we are good skeptics, lurks the dreaded will to power and the possibility of betraying our virtue for a taste of blood. We have grown forever distrustful of our own motives. We know that the enemy is within. Only by identifying with a purer consciousness, an otherness, might we cleanse ourselves of our pitiful humanity, its vulgar interests, and the will to dominate, although it can never be certain whether this ideal of otherness, usually associated with the powerless, the voice of the victim, minorities, the third world, and women, contains our longed-for perfection and the freedom from violence. What is clear is that we desire to identify ourselves with a world in which the powerless reign. Which is to say that we want to live in a time diametrically opposed to our own era, in which power has asserted itself with unrivaled visibility in the two World Wars, in Korea, in Vietnam, in the race for space, in charismatic tyrants and corrupt politicians, and in the might of nuclear weapons. We have lived for almost half a century with the

---

[22] The example of Lyotard stands out from all the others here. See Jean-François Lyotard, *The Differend: Phrases in Dispute,* trans. Georges Van Den Abbeele (Minneapolis: University of Minnesota Press, 1988). For an excellent comparison of Rawls and Lyotard on justice, see Charles Altieri, "Judgement and Justice Under Postmodern Conditions: Or How Lyotard Helps Us Read Rawls as a Postmodern Thinker," in his *Canons and Consequences,* chapter 9.

possibility that Longinus's fantasy of sublime power could become a reality: "the world set afire with deeds of evil." Rather than living with this fire, this threat, this power, or doing something about it, we have preferred to remain frozen, paralyzed by cold war skepticism and hesitancy. The apparent antidote to the world set afire is Dante's Satan. We have locked ourselves in a prison of ice.

A persistent theme of the skeptical criticism of the postwar era has been the necessity of standing against belief, conformity, authority, systems, conventions, and institutions, whether in the form of national hegemonies, canons, schools of thought, or constructions of race, gender, and class. I have been arguing that our perception of the violence of totality, authority, and systems of belief has been tainted directly by our experience with cold war politics. But it is worth considering how strange it is that the skeptical criticism of this period has experienced such a remarkable success at the institutional level. Recent presidents of the Modern Language Association have included J. Hillis Miller and Barbara Hernstein Smith, skeptical critics both, and statistics collected by the Modern Language Association reveal that Derrida is the most footnoted author in the humanities of the last twenty years. If skeptical criticism is so fiercely antagonistic to our institutions, so adverse, why has it been so successful? Perhaps its success is due to its general sympathy to cold war attitudes. In this case, it may be valuable to review the ideas, attitudes, and methods that recent criticism has spent so much energy rejecting. The foundation of a post–cold war criticism may well reside in the taboo words of a generation of cold war critics—the self, inner life, soul, emotion, emancipation, trust, communication, altruism, love, responsibility, belief, religion, community, citizenship, culture, beauty, harmony, knowledge, truth—and in their attendant disciplines: psychology, ethics, anthropology, aesthetics, and the sciences. The task facing modern criticism, and it is dubious whether skeptical criticism can accomplish it, is not to preserve literature from destruction by world politics but to create a politics of literature that is at home in the world.

3

Ethics or Politics? Comparative Literature, Multiculturalism, and Cultural Literacy

The history of comparative literature has never been free of controversy. The discipline of comparative literature began as an attempt to define the specific nature of literature apart from the constraints of national and linguistic boundaries, but this attempt soon became embroiled in the ethics and politics of nationalism. Two distinct trends were apparent during the early years of comparative literature.[1] The concept of "world" or "general" literature was used by comparatists to attack chauvinism among nations and to expose nationalistic myths. Thus, Carré and Guyard included within the province of comparative literature the study of national illusions. At the same time, however, influence studies allowed nationalism to gain a secure foothold in comparative literature, and critics began to take special pride in the discovery that their national writers had a major impact on another nation's great authors. Thus, we heard talk about the Byronism of Pushkin or Baudelaire's debt to Poe. Comparatists also delighted in the belief that they had come to understand another nation's tradition

[1] For the history of comparative literature, I have relied on the accounts of Ulrich Weisstein, *Comparative Literature and Literary Theory* (Bloomington: Indiana University Press, 1973), 167–252, and René Wellek, "The Crisis of Comparative Literature," in his *Concepts of Criticism* (New Haven, Conn.: Yale University Press, 1963), 282–95.

better than it had itself, resulting in conquests in letters rather than on land.

Another early theoretical development seemed to have less obvious effects on the ethics of critical theory, but it possesses an unexpected pertinence for the current scene. Both Van Tieghem and Baldensperger argued that comparative literature should concern itself specifically with minor authors. It may be a considerable jump from this emphasis to the idea of a "minor literature," but any examination of present canon theory among comparatists will lead to the conclusion that more than a family resemblance unites the early comparatists' desire to examine minor authors and the current practice of emphasizing the literature of minority groups and third world nations. The concern with minor authors, especially among feminists, has had a great impact on the limited domain of canon formation; and the concern with minority groups and third world nations is overtly ethical in its attempt to redesign the canon to conform to a "more perfect" map of the world. It is clear, however, that the desire for inclusiveness present in the former finds its culmination in the refusal to exclude in the latter, and that the obvious ethical intentions of a minor literature resonate on a smaller scale in the desire to read minor authors. Both projects obey the comparatist's demand that literature be considered a unified human activity, exempt from divisions of nation, class, race, and gender; but it is perhaps less obvious that they are also motivated by an ideal of social unanimity, since both intend to create a perfectly coherent human community from which no one is excluded.

Apart from the idea that literature is best studied as a human activity, and not as the practice of a specific nation or group, comparative literature's greatest contribution has been to make us more aware of the social dimension of literary criticism. Whether the ability of comparative literature to bring about this awareness should be called political or ethical, however, is an issue worthy of debate. The current scene obscures the importance of distinguishing between politics and ethics for reasons that I will discuss in a moment, but it remains crucial to broach this question because many of the motivations behind recent debates over multiculturalism, cultural literacy, and canon formation make little sense if we take a monolithic view of the ethico-political.

There are not, for example, many political reasons for championing the literatures of other nations; and those that come to mind serve the kind of politics that most humanistic scholars would abhor. It is valuable, we might be told, to study the literature of other nations for the purpose of understanding their history and psychology; such knowledge might prove useful in political and business negotiations. But students of literature usually find such reasoning, based on realpolitiks and the bottom line, to be a crass betrayal of the specific joys and lessons given by the literary text. We would rather literature had no utility at all than see it used in this manner. Indeed, many theorists insist on literature's lack of utility precisely in order to free themselves from the clash of the world. One imagines in this regard the spectacle of the major aesthetic thinkers of Europe casting their eyes on the French Revolution and trying with all their might to save art from the burgeoning chaos. Aesthetic theory matured on a world stage characterized by violence and brutality, and yet it managed to shun any hint of social involvement. Small wonder, then, that Kantian "disinterestedness" and "purposelessness" became the accepted way of describing art, for only this view was capable of untangling aesthetics from the violence of contemporary history. In a real sense, the notion that beauty is the symbol of morality translates into the unfortunate opinion that humanity can possess the moral only in the domain of representation; the aesthetic community has lost hope of achieving it in the real world.

Whenever we question the objection to a political use of literature, then, we can expect to hear an appeal of some kind to a higher ideal, most likely to the ethical ideal demanding that we respect diversity and individuality. The political has been tainted by human violence, and "literature" is supposed by many critics to be the cure for violence. I think it even more probable that we would hear this ethical appeal from comparatists for the simple reason that they have been taught to ignore political expediency in favor of a more international and ideal worldview.[2] The apparent "politics" of comparative literature, then, is

[2] Comparatists often present comparative literature as a solution to disciplinary and political fragmentation. For them, literature provides the model for utopian social and academic organization. To sample this attitude, see Jean-Pierre Barricelli and Joseph

really an ethical doctrine, which is not to say that it has no ideal polity
in mind. It is only to say that this polity is more abstract than real, less
practical than theoretical. Comparative literature as a discipline has
taken on the burden of symbolizing the moral. Against the desire for
political and national coherence dramatized on the world stage, the
ethics of comparative literature opposes a symbolic and wholly inclusive human activity named "literature," and this "literature" serves as
the metaphor of communal totality.

It is not at all certain, however, that the issues are so clear-cut or that
either comparative literature or multiculturalism holds the solution to
all our social woes. The rise of cultural relativisim has successfully
transformed "nationalism" into a derogatory concept, but some people of late have argued that it can be a positive attitude, especially
when used to build the confidence of peoples who have been historically oppressed. On the one hand, the role played by literature in
defining national characteristics has obvious political benefits because
it tends to support patriotism and national pride. On the other hand,
the apparent exclusion of other traditions from literary canons seems
to fly in the face of the ethical view that multiculturalism, world citi-

---

Gibaldi, eds., *Interrelations of Literature* (New York: Modern Language Association,
1982), where it is argued:

> Primarily under the aegis of comparative literature, the study of letters has become
> progressively more interdisciplinary as well as interliterary. Through this impor-
> tant development in modern scholarship, literature is being restored to its pristine
> position as a central cognitive resource in society, as its most faithful and compre-
> hensive interpreter. It is an art but more than an art, for, while being itself, litera-
> ture extends outside itself to forms of human experience beyond disciplinary
> boundaries, making it evident that the rigid separation of disciplines by myopic
> specializations can in the long run lead only to counterproductive and paralyzing
> isolation. Literature, as the hub of the wheel of knowledge, provides the logical
> locus for the integration of knowledge. (iv)

Jonathan Culler, "Comparative Literature and the Pieties," *Profession* (1986):
30–32, also favors enthroning the cosmopolitan values of comparative literature
to eliminate the provincialism of religious belief. For an intelligent reading
of this phenomenon in terms of the relation between literature and scientific research, see Paisley Livingston, *Literary Knowledge: Humanistic Inquiry
and the Philosophy of Science* (Ithaca, N.Y.: Cornell University Press, 1988),
19–20.

zenship, and human difference are not only valuable in the modern world but required if we are to have any reasonable hope for the survival of the human species.

What I am trying to delimit is the delicate relation between ethics and politics. The relation between ethics and politics is highly charged, and, in the modern period especially, we may have difficulties positing the unity and disunity between them. When we do consider their relation, we usually err on the side of idealism, arguing that ethics should have nothing to do with politics. This position is ironic, since a truly idealistic vision would seem more likely to favor a state where politics and ethics converge, such as Aristotle described. The problem, however, is that the modern world is wholly disillusioned with ethics and utterly distrustful of politics, and it cannot bear to think of the two together.

If Aristotle was correct, however, the ethical and the political should not differ considerably, and when they differ, it should be largely in the nature of the community that they address.[3] The ethical aspires to a wholly inclusive community, and is therefore oriented toward the future and possesses a more theoretical and abstract dimension. It is interested in the realm of practice, although its notion of practice might be better described as an essentially hypothetical operation geared toward obtaining an ideal state of human cohesiveness. The political also aspires to a wholly inclusive community, but it exercises itself on a community already in existence and therefore tends to restrict itself to the temporal and geographical limitations of that particular community. It struggles to discover how it may affect a specific group, but it strives at every turn to preserve this group against other political bodies. It is possible, therefore, to create political alliances, whereas it does not make any sense to speak of ethical alliances, for politics concerns the relation between essential and distinct groups, and ethics believes that ultimately there should be only one group. Whence the necessity that Kant take as a given the existence of a community of rational beings, before turning to a description of the categorical imperative.

[3] These matters are a persistent concern in my *Morals and Stories* (New York: Columbia University Press, 1992), esp. chapters 2, 9, 12, and 13.

Feminist politics provides a case in point. It may seem contradictory, for instance, that the feminist movement, especially in France and among separatists, argues for an essential feminine difference, when such beliefs are arguably the cause of the historical disenfranchisement of women. History suggests that women would want to demonstrate their parity with men, and, of course, this happens often enough; but, as many radical feminists have claimed, capitulating to mainstream culture does not gain political power. It is first necessary to solidify a political group before it can make demands, and the argument for feminine difference begins the work of creating just such a political faction. The local and necessary politics of feminism therefore appears to contradict its larger ethical quest for equality, but if feminism does not "risk" essentialism it will never have a voice in determining its own destiny.[4] I call this politics risky because it mirrors the male factionalism that it opposes, and it consequently risks reproducing the same kinds of inequities. Moreover, there is no guarantee that feminists will have the courage to dismantle their own rhetoric when the time comes to reject political factionalism and to build a more coherent society with men, although, personally, I remain optimistic.

It is not to be expected that these distinctions between politics and ethics are hard and fast, and I propose them merely to make a beginning from which to discuss some of the factionalism currently troubling theories of literature and education. In fact, the task of distinguishing between the ethical and the political is extremely difficult, and for at least two reasons. First, as I already noted, "politics" is a negative concept within critical theory today: every criticism is political, we are informed, but these politics are always ferociously ideological and always of a kind that we would be better to do without. Indeed, thanks to the cold war, we take it for granted that we would be lucky to be totally free of politics. It may be a virture to read literature politically, that is, to demystify an opponent's politics; but it goes without saying that someone else will be able to expose my ideology. The politics of interpretation reminds one of the Wild West: no matter how political a critic may be, there is always someone more political; there is always a

[4]I analyze the ethics of sexual difference at greater length in *The Ethics of Criticism* (Ithaca, N.Y.: Cornell University Press, 1988), chapter 8.

faster gun. In short, the politics of interpretation is marked by the kind of competition and power plays that its supporters find so abhorrent in politics as such, especially those of the cold war years.

Indeed, there are surprisingly few ways to be politically correct on the current scene. Marxists claim to be politically correct, but only Marxists believe that they are successful. Marxist critics used to expose ideology for a living, but when the term "ideology" gained broader usage it was turned against them (and everyone else), so that we may now refer to "Marxist ideology." Today everyone has his or her ideology, and no two ideologies need be the same. Universals no longer exist, which is perhaps the great difference between the claims of politics and ethics, aside from the issue of practice.

For cold war critics, ethics ends by being less trustworthy than politics. Its domain cannot even be established without raising skepticism. Any time we try to separate politics and ethics, we commit a crime because the gesture is associated with a political and ideological tactic designed to mask ideology. To say that one's motivations are ethical, and not political, is viewed as the political statement par excellence. Indeed, one result of the growing suspicion of politics in the postwar world has been the reduction of all social thought to mere politics; ethics is now commonly described as a strategic language designed to hide political intentions. Perhaps, the only ethical statement is to admit that one is always political, meaning that one is always on the brink of immorality; ethical thought is thereby reduced to the moral attitude that René Girard calls "equalization in villainy."[5] In short, cold war thought recognizes the inseparability of ethics and politics but only in its negative moment, when they arise as rival terms. We cannot imagine a positive unity between them any more than we can imagine how they might legitimately differ. We have not conserved the sense, for example, that the Greeks had of the rapport between ethics and politics, in which any ethics referred by definition to a polis for which its moral propositions must be thought valid.

I have already implied the second reason why we have difficulty separating ethics and politics. Each term plays the villain for the other,

[5] René Girard, "Hamlet's Dull Revenge," *Stanford Literature Review* 1, no. 2 (1984): 159–200.

and this equalization in villainy makes distinctions problematic. In Aristotle's terms, no polis is above suspicion, and therefore no ethics can be other than merely political, that is, designed specifically to satisfy the chauvinism of one group. We should note that this attitude does not hide a romantic disdain for the group because we view individual behavior in the same light: individuals are just as untrustworthy as groups when it comes to ethical claims.[6] Ethical language, as defined by cold war theory, always conceals the will to power; it rationalizes for others our most selfish desires.

Given the history of comparative literature, and its preoccupation with the politics of nationalism, it is no accident that it holds the conceptual center in current debates over the value of a literary education, multiculturalism, and cultural literacy. It is equally important to recognize that this debate is made all the more confusing by our present tendency to view politics and ethics as rival terms. Allan Bloom's *Closing of the American Mind,* for example, attacks cultural relativism as the villain that has robbed the American spirit of its sense of self, and in Bloom's eyes the embodiment of cultural relativism is comparative literature.[7] Time after time he names comparative literature as the haven for relativists, multiculturalists, detractors of American education, and celebrants of unreason. For the main agenda of comparative literature, according to Bloom, has been to deny the possibility of truth and knowledge in order to liberate the creative energy of the inter-

[6] Part of the current dislike of politics may be traced to the rejection of group organization begun during the romantic period and climaxing during the last quarter of the nineteenth century with the invention of criminal anthropology. We usually read romanticism in terms of its excessive lyricism and individualism, but the other side of the coin, of course, reveals a loss of confidence in social order. One wonders, in fact, whether romantic individualism is not initially motivated by the desire to escape the violence of politics by taking shelter in the temple of the self. This desire, of course, finds its fulfillment in psychoanalysis, where, to twist a modern phrase, the personal becomes the political.

[7] References are to Allan Bloom, *The Closing of the American Mind: Education and the Crisis of Reason* (New York: Simon and Schuster, 1987). Dinesh D'Souza also singles out comparative literature as a source of trouble in academia. His complaints about the English department at Duke University really amount to displeasure with the fact that it has switched its emphasis from traditional texts of English literature to a more comparatist and multicultural menu. See Dinesh D'Souza, *Illiberal Education: The Politics of Race and Sex on Campus* (New York: Free Press, 1991).

preter. This doctrine explains that there is no text and no reality, only individual interpretation, and its value resides in its ability to express the interpreter's freedom.

Bloom's complaint will be familiar to those who have taught literary theory in recent years. But it is important to note that he does not have the usual reasons for opposing critical theory. We need only ask what group he represents to understand why he believes that multicultural-ism is risky. Bloom believes that classical education in general and the American cultural experience in particular have been endangered by the ethic of cultural relativism. He sets himself up to defend American democracy and the tradition of classical learning from those who would dilute the former with foreign ideas and fragment the latter by asserting that knowledge is relative to political contexts. For Bloom, therefore, nationalism has its good sides, and the hegemony of classical texts, hegemony though it may be, is still central to the best that has been thought and said. Any attempt to challenge these tenets will endanger the cohesiveness of the political group that Bloom has chosen to champion.

On the other hand, comparative literature has recently spawned a new interest in ethics, and its theorists inhabit the very camp that Bloom views as scandalous. "Ethics" has become a buzz word among "Parisian Heideggerians" and "deconstructionists" here and abroad, to use Bloom's labels; and various commentators on literary theory, J. Hillis Miller for one, have begun to ask about the ethics of literary interpretation. Miller's *Ethics of Reading* takes a position that would seem at first to be diametrically opposed to that of Bloom.[8] Indeed, Miller's heroes are the European "nihilists" whom Bloom detests, and

[8] J. Hillis Miller has written two essays under the title of "The Ethics of Reading" an early exploratory essay, "The Ethics of Reading: Vast Gaps and Parting Hours," in *American Criticism in the Poststructuralist Age,* ed. Ira Konigsberg (Ann Arbor: University of Michigan Press, 1981), 19–41, and the later monograph *The Ethics of Reading* (New York: Columbia University Press, 1987). References to the essay ("ER") and to the book (*ER*) will be given parenthetically in the text. A sequel to the latter, *Versions of Pygmalion* (Cambridge, Mass.: Harvard University Press, 1990), continues the reading assignment with little change in theory. For an extended analysis of Miller's position in the context of linguistic ethics, see my *Morals and Stories* (New York: Columbia University Press, 1992), chapter 3. On *Versions of Pygmalion,* see my "Reading for Character: Where It Was, I Must Come to Be," *Semiotica* (forthcoming).

Miller returns again and again to the wisdom of Nietzsche and Freud. His reading of Kant, for example, begins and ends in Freudianisms, speaking of "interminable analysis" and "slips of the tongue," although it is not clear that Kant can be read from a Freudian perspective without severely distorting his position. Miller's strategy of reading is both conservative and radical. It seems conservative on first glance because he argues for a strict obedience to the text. His "linguistic imperative" is to allow the text to take place and to read its necessity. The text is the law, and it is our duty to obey it and to allow it to coerce us. On second glance, Miller's strategy looks radical because he claims that interpretation as we know it cannot produce anything meaningful.

It is revealing, however, to compare Miller on textuality with George Will's reading of Bloom. According to Miller, "the ethics of reading is not some act of the human will to interpretation which extracts moral themes from a work, or uses it to reaffirm what the reader already knows, or imposes a meaning freely in some process of reader response or perspectivist criticism, seeing the text in a certain way. The ethics of reading is the power of the words of the text over the mind and words of the reader" ("ER," 41). Similarly, as George Will sees it, "pedagogy that focuses on the social context that supposedly produced and explains the text's significance, rather than on the text itself, elevates the professor unduly. It places him in the grand—too grand—role of the supplier of social theories which are supposedly indispensable for interpretation of the texts. Thus today's teachers with their agendas, not the texts, become the sources of illumination."[9]

Miller does not seem to be quilty of the frivolous invention of which Bloom accuses comparatists and multiculturalists, and we might soon expect to see his byline next to Will's in the pages of *Newsweek*. Bloom, Will, and Miller appear to share the same distrust of political agendas; they prefer an ethics of reading that privileges "great" literature. Bloom believes that we should submit ourselves to Plato's *Republic* and obey the Socratic creed. Will laments changes in Stanford's

[9] George Will, "Politics of Stanford Debate Troublesome," *Ann Arbor News,* 3 May 1988, A–13.

"great books" program. Miller makes it clear that he is searching for an ethical moment in the act of reading, "a moment neither cognitive, nor political, nor social, nor interpersonal, but properly and independently ethical" (ER, 1). Indeed, Miller sees a gulf separating the ethical and the political: "No doubt the political and ethical are always intimately intertwined, but an ethical act that is fully determined by political considerations or responsibilities is no longer ethical. It could even in a certain sense be said to be amoral" (ER, 4). For Miller the ethical moment is sui generis, autonomously determined by itself, a cause rather than an effect of political conduct.

How do we account for the family resemblance between such false cousins as Bloom and Miller? Each would appear to represent what the other most detests, and yet they seem to share basic premises about textuality and the evils of educational demagoguery. One problem, of course, is that we do not possess a clear vocabulary for dealing with political and ethical issues in literary theory, and consequently we do not have an easy means of distinguishing the nature of the various claims made in their name. Usually, the mere mention of the word "politics" is enough to situate one left of center, whereas only the most conservative of critics tend to make reference to ethics.

The case here is quite the opposite, for Bloom's political analysis serves the right, and most would tend to identify Miller with the avantgarde, despite the fact that he is a former president of the Modern Language Association and has rarely, if ever, strayed from the traditional literary canon in his own writings. According to Miller, the text requires that we read it in a particular way, without subjecting it to extrinsic forces; but this does not mean that our reading will result in a form of political order, unless it is the order of disorder. For Miller reminds us in the words of Paul de Man that "it is forever impossible to read Reading" (ER, 47). In other words, the text demands that we impose no meaning on it and that we read it apart from our own requirements; but the nature of language in Miller's estimation is such that we will find no meaning apart from that which we impose. Reading, according to Miller and de Man, is the art of resisting our impulses to impose meaning, to decide the text, when no such act is possible. "The failure to read or the impossibility of reading," Miller asserts, "is a universal necessity, one moment of which is the potentially aberrant form of language called ethical judgment or prescription" (*ER*, 51). Only when language becomes an aberration do we find ethics as traditionally defined. The only true ethical response is the skeptical one, in which thought strips itself of inferior constructions: Miller works to separate ethics from politics and to adhere to an ethics now defined as the resistance to anything ethical or political. The perfected form of this ethics is linguistic structure itself, and "literature" accepts the burden of symbolizing, without reference to the social world, the apotheosis of the moral.

The Ethics of Reading is supposed to be a response to those critics of deconstruction who argue that the movement is nihilistic. But "nihilism" is not the right term to describe Miller's textual theories, unless we give it a special meaning. Nihilism embraces no creed, but this is not Miller's problem. Miller is a believer in a certain linguistic creed, and he obeys its principles with great strictness. Yet there may be cause to confuse his approach with nihilism, if we consider the moral justifications usually given for believing in nothing. Believing in nothing is thought to be more ethical than believing in something because belief, according to cold war skeptics, usually leads directly to confrontation on the battlefield.

Miller's book enacts this same logic but with an interesting twist. He takes a strong position, but the position is such that no position may result from it. He cannot, therefore, represent any political group effectively, unless he contradicts his own theories, and ethically speaking, he supports the idea that no community or set of propositions can ever be constituted that will not be hopelessly immoral. The ethical community created by his theories is therefore ferociously and purposely nonexistent. Skepticism always constructs its ethics by creating a position where it is impossible to stand. Like Paul de Man, Miller ends by arguing that the perfect ethical moment may take place only in the absence of human intervention. Whereas Kant posits the existence of a community of rational beings as the first step in the creation of his critical ethics, Miller's first maneuver is to outlaw the desire for any such totality.

This is why the claim that *The Ethics of Reading* demonstrates the political or ethical responsibility of deconstruction will not hold water. Miller likes to talk about responsibility, but there are no concrete positions in the book, not even the faintest suggestions about the ethics of teaching or classroom practices. The only examples of ethical practice are his literary interpretations, but his readings do not differ essentially from any number currently found on the library shelves. The merit of Miller's book—its great merit but its only merit—resides in his general claim that literature and ethics do have something to do with each other. But this is a long way from proving one's particular ethical responsibility. In fact, Miller's theories are neither responsible nor irresponsible: they are determinedly apolitical and amoral. By his definition, there can be no lesson in literature for the practice of either ethics or politics, for the desire for such lessons is in itself the greatest political and moral failure. All that remains is to obey a linguistic imperative that affirms the ethical and political undecidability, that is, the neutrality, of language itself.[10]

A book such as *The Closing of the American Mind* must by Miller's lights succumb precisely to the temptation to look for political lessons in literature. For Bloom names particular texts that teach us about political life. On this specific question I find Bloom's view more palatable, but I do not want to suggest that I agree with his account of American education. Literature, I think, can have no claim to significance in our age unless it has value for understanding human conduct, and Bloom at least makes it possible to consider the value of literature; but his politics are too defensive, and ultimately too closed. One may

[10] This tactic amounts to what I would call ethical hygiene, in which the agent attempts to identify his or her position with that of pure language because language itself supposedly represents a state of perfect ethical form. It is another version of the skeptic's desire to purify thought of its poorer versions in order to achieve apotheosis. Miller, in fact, ascribes to the metaphor of hygiene in an address cited by John Sutherland in *TLS* 13, no. 1 (1991): 3–6, where he recommends "that we should give up the attempt to transfer ethical themes directly from literature to life" and that "departments of literature should reduce their function to a kind of linguistic hygiene—that is, to a study of the rhetoric of literature, what might be called 'literariness'" (5–6). It is perhaps worth remarking, in the context of my emerging argument that radical literary criticism often replays a cold war agenda against the new counterculture values of the sixties, that Miller's doctrine of "linguistic hygiene" mirrors the conservative response to the counterculture.

respect, for example, his reading of the black power movement of the 1960s as a critique of violence, but as an allegory of the fall of the American university it is profoundly disturbing. Too often everything detrimental to American thought is identified by Bloom with African-American culture: American education is toppled by black politics, and rock-and-roll music saps the spirit of our youth by confusing their minds with the beat of sexual intercourse. We should remember here that the earliest detractors of rock music opposed it precisely because of its black influences. Bloom's title is, in the final analysis, more indicative of his own designs for American education than of any effect produced by the so-called intervention of alien ideas. He would have us close our minds and universities to internationalism, multiculturalism, and modernist thought in order to preserve a national spirit and the traditional canon.

But no such militant action may be necessary. While I am equally concerned about the future of American education, especially as I reflect on what the students in my classroom know, the only action that I would recommend is that teachers get down to the business of teaching our students what they ought to know. I add quickly that I remain insistently naive in the belief that teachers do know what ought to be taught, even though they may sometimes disagree on its significance and political slant. E. D. Hirsch has made a convincing argument for the importance of "cultural literacy," which means that teachers must provide students with the background information necessary to understand the subtleties of literature and the world.[11] His idea is useful—as long as we avoid the pop versions that he has recently introduced—because it reminds us that sophisticated cultural analysis and literary theory must be preceded by an identification and understanding of the basic ideas of our society. This does not have to mean that we should close the doors of the classroom to everything that does not belong to American or Western culture, but we do have the responsibility to give our students a comprehension of what it means to live where they live and of what their relation is to other cultures. We can

[11] E. D. Hirsch, Jr., *Cultural Literacy: What Every American Needs to Know* (Boston: Houghton Mifflin, 1987). Hirsch's more recent efforts, encyclopedias of facts and quizzes for Yuppie consumption, are not worth mentioning.

expect no less of non-Western classrooms, which may well wish, for example, to defend an initial resistance to "Americanisms" as a way of giving students a good sense of their own traditions.

Too often cultural relativism provides the excuse to escape teaching responsibilities that professionals find tedious but that students require as basic information. It is perhaps no accident that the idea of cultural relativism evolved in the context of colonial adventurism, for it continues to serve people who prefer forays into exoticism over teaching basic ideas about their own society. It also serves to justify theoretical pronouncements about the world at large by teachers who may not have any experience beyond their own backyards.[12] Theorists frequently act as if their courses were ends in themselves, claiming to provide the secret code that will unravel the mysteries of language, literature, and culture. Their grandiose claims are rarely, if ever, supported by any form of proof, and they usually serve an excess of personal vanity and professional rivalry rather than a knowledge of the subjects. These classrooms operate like little sovereign states, declaring their opposition to the rest of the curriculum. But, in fact, the excitement that they generate is fueled not by learning but by a spirit of revolt and aggression against everything surrounding them. The theories of literature and cultural analysis commonly found in our classrooms today are attractive, and I believe necessary, but they should be taught for their own merit at the proper time and by the proper people and not to make teaching more amusing for professors. If there is an essential ethic of teaching, it is the requirement that a teacher leave his or her students in such a state of knowledge that they may continue their education after they leave his or her teaching behind. Good teachers know the relation between their subjects and those of their colleagues; and they do not pretend that their courses alone are the keys to what other people are thinking and saying. Good teachers

[12] An anecdote that is both amusing and unsettling: Now that cultural studies and postcolonial criticism have emerged as area studies in much demand, the rush to qualify as expert in them has grown rather feverishly. In the last two years I have sat on two search committees for such positions, and it is not at all uncommon to read application letters in which candidates, who have written dissertations on Jane Austen and William Shakespeare, claim a powerful enthusiasm and growing awareness about cultural studies as a result of having spent a two-week vacation in the Caribbean.

dispense both their own strong opinions and the opinions of others as well as the facts. To use the classroom for one's own narcissism, personal amusement, private agendas, or political mission transgresses the ethics of teaching and undermines the student's confidence.

The great advantage of comparative literature and multiculturalism is their requirement that literature be read at the crossroads of nations and times. For being at the crossroads provides opportunities for reflecting on the mix of ideas and opinions. To assert that comparatists must interpret only on the margins of culture, searching for minor texts and authors, severely limits this natural advantage, although we should always be on the lookout to recover what has been displaced by the grand rush of ideas. As any good comparatist knows, reading a work of literature requires a fundamental knowledge of the history of its country of origin, the national literature surrounding it, and its cultural milieu, before the work of interpretation may begin.

The ongoing brouhaha over "great books" and the politics of multiculturalism, for example, misunderstands the nature of interpretation and demonstrates just how confused are our ideas of politics and literature on both the right and left. Conservatives believe that multiculturalism is responsible for the apparent decline in American education, considering it un-American, overly political, and so forth. But the politics of multiculturalism is at the heart of American pluralism and its myth of the melting pot. The danger in multiculturalism, if there is any, lies in its skeptical contempt for genuine politics; skepticism is utopian in its desire to achieve new democratic forms outside the political process. Here canon revision serves a symbolic function because it represents certain canons as indicative of evil politics and others as indicative of good politics. Similarly, the conservative embrace of "great books" represents certain canons as a symbol of a harmonious West, whose unity and prominence must be preserved at all costs. But these books come from many different cultures and periods and hardly represent a unity; indeed, a first reading of them requires one to confront the fact of their diversity. Good classicists, for instance, know that Homer's world is not our world, and they are aware of the act of translation by which we use his thinking to reflect on our own society. The serious study of literature requires an awareness of both the otherness and the relevance of specific works, a fact that both radicals and conservatives fail to understand. In the final analysis, then, radicals and conservatives are equally utopian in their belief that works of literature in themselves and uninterpreted preserve political bodies.

It is interpretation, however, that produces the value of literary works for political communities. Literature needs to be read and read again to have its political effects; and Toni Morrison may be as valuable as Homer in this interpretive process. Indeed, we cannot read Morrison without knowing Homer, and it seems clear at this moment that we cannot read Homer without knowing Morrison. Only "theory" conceives of a politics purified of this interpretive work, and the right and the left alike take an overly theoretical approach to the politics of literature.

More important, perhaps, the good comparatist and multiculturalist should have an appreciation for both the frivolity and the usefulness of the accidents of literary interpretation, for not every connection between texts is a deliberate allusion or influence, although every one of them may be significant for an understanding of how literature fits into the scheme of human action and thought. In the last analysis, the biggest problem with the theories of Bloom and Miller is that they are afraid of accidents. For Bloom, the accidental signifies the invasion of foreign ideas and the disruption of our cultural heritage; for Miller, the accidental is the disquieting ripple of humanity disturbing the tranquil surface of language. Both exchange the perils of an open society, in which people are free to share ideas and opinions, for the security of a closed system.

We should value American higher education because it gives freedom to students and teachers alike. There are many opportunities to have one's say and to teach and to learn what one considers important. This freedom necessarily produces accidents, perhaps even catastrophes, in the educational process. But an open society must accept accidents as one of the essential conditions of its existence, and the more we learn to accept accidents and to pick ourselves up after collisions, the better our society will be. The curriculum of the American university changed during the 1960s; it will change again. The important thing to remember is that we have both a past and a future; such is the necessary union of politics and ethics in any intelligent society.

4

Mourning Becomes Paul de Man

Paul de Man's *Allegories of Reading* defines one of its major terms, "rhetoric," as "a *text* in that it allows for two incompatible, mutually self-destructive points of view, and therefore puts an insurmountable obstacle in the way of any reading or understanding" (131).[1] Language is always rhetorical in de Man's mind; metaphor is not an aberrant form of language but "the linguistic paradigm par excellence" (105). De Man likens his theory of language to Nietzsche's early writings on rhetoric, those writings that established Nietzsche as one of the three masters of suspicion and the progenitor of modern deconstruction, and he takes pains to exhume the most skeptical formulations from Nietzsche's notes: "No such thing as an unrhetorical, 'natural' language exists that could be used as a point of reference: language is itself the result of purely rhetorical tricks and devices . . ." (105).

When brought into the orbit of Nietzsche's later writings, the rhetorical nature of language becomes a symptom of the will to power, one of the many tactics of persuasion by which the will asserts itself over truth. As a result, all knowledge of the self would appear to be a rhetoric of error destined to further the aims of individual power and

---

[1] References are to Paul de Man, "Genesis and Genealogy," "Rhetoric of Tropes," and "Rhetoric of Persuasion," in his *Allegories of Reading* (New Haven, Conn.: Yale University Press, 1979), 79–102, 103–18, 119–34, respectively.

will. The self is itself a construction of rhetoric. De Man defines truth as the persistence of error and finds that Nietzsche as well as Proust, Rousseau, and Rilke affirm the fact. The epigraph to *Blindness and Insight,* "Cette perpétuelle erreur, qui est précisément la 'vie' . . . ,'' although taken from Proust, nevertheless comes to summarize more and more de Man's view of Nietzsche and his skeptical vision of life. Ultimately, for de Man language takes on the features of a prison-house, and the formation of the self becomes more a question of rhetorical construction than of ethics, politics, or psychology. "If you want to talk about men, you are in the wrong field," de Man is imputed to have responded to criticism of his views. "We can only talk about letters."[2]

De Man admits that his approach may be farfetched and oblique because rhetoric appears by all evidence to be an "eccentric and minor part of Nietzsche's enterprise" (103). Deconstruction relies on the now-classic technique of reinscribing the major term of an argument, here the "self," within its minor one, here "rhetoric"; and the result in this case is the desired exorbitancy of de Man's theory of rhetoric. But once the major term, "self," is marginalized, does it not risk returning in the deconstructive project to reassert its value? And what would the deconstruction of a deconstructive argument be? Either it is the most radical form of deconstruction because it always asserts its conscious preference for the minor term, despite previous deconstructions or traditional values, or it is the most conservative of criticisms.

Such would be a few questions posed by de Man's rhetoric of the self, and his writings on Nietzsche in particular provide the occasion for further inquiry. Nietzsche, of course, knew a great deal about the strategic potential of skepticism, marginality, and loss; in fact, his theory of resentment demonstrates that personal power can be built on the loss of power. Deconstruction in de Man's hands imitates the philosophy of resentment, fracturing the binary logic of major and minor to engage in a Nietzschean game in which the skeptical self wins power by mourning its own loss. Consequently, de Man's writings on the interference between rhetoric and selfhood return inevitably to

[2] Cited in Stephen J. Greenblatt, ed., *Allegory and Representation* (Baltimore: Johns Hopkins University Press, 1981), viii.

Nietzsche, running from the early "Literary History and Literary Modernity" in *Blindness and Insight,* to the three chapters on Nietzschean theory at the heart of *Allegories of Reading,* and finally to the late reading of Nietzsche and Baudelaire in *The Rhetoric of Romanticism.* It is in de Man's reading of Nietzsche's caustic skepticism and preoccupation with resentment that we may begin to understand his own views on rhetoric and selfhood and to anticipate their relation to his politics.

My suspicion that de Man's work comes into its own in response to Nietzsche is confirmed by the fact that "Literary History and Literary Modernity" gives a different view of Nietzsche and only suggests de Man's late views on rhetoric.[3] The strategy of *Blindness and Insight* is largely skeptical: it tests the limits of knowledge by demonstrating that critical insights are gained from a "negative movement" that eventually leads their language away from their assertions and empties them of substance. In the case of Nietzsche, the limitation of thought arises in the apparent division between the ideas of "history" and "modernity." De Man claims that Nietzsche views modernity as an ahistorical mentality that seeks to blot out historical consciousness as a prerequisite to action, but as soon as modernity becomes conscious of itself, de Man argues, it reveals its dependence on history, and Nietzsche's insight dissolves. "Nietzsche," de Man concludes, "finds it impossible to escape from history, and he finally has to bring the two incompatibles, history and modernity (now using the term in the full sense of a radical renewal), together in a paradox that cannot be resolved, an aporia . . ." (150).

De Man's reading of Nietzsche focuses on the limits of one man's thought, on how the nature of language, in effect, becomes an obstacle to his understanding. The late de Man would never make such a strange claim; rather, he argues that literary language by its very nature makes understanding difficult because it subverts its own assertions. Language possesses its own insights and blindness. The elements of this late position, however, are already present in the first book, especially in "The Rhetoric of Blindness," where de Man criticizes

[3] References are to Paul de Man, "Literary History and Literary Modernity," in his *Blindness and Insight* (Minneapolis: University of Minnesota Press, 1983), 142–65.

Derrida's idea that Rousseau has to be deconstructed at all. To deconstruct Rousseau's text, de Man reasons, would be to assume a position of superiority with regard to it. De Man believes that Rousseau's language already does to itself what Derrida works to achieve in his reading. "The Rhetoric of Blindness" immediately precedes "Literary History and Literary Modernity," perhaps giving the reader the false impression that Rousseau's writing is a special case: whereas Rousseau deconstructs himself, Nietzsche apparently needs to be deconstructed. If one were to write a subtitle for de Man's essay on Nietzsche, with an understanding of the late theories, it would have to be: "Where De Man Does to Nietzsche What He Says Derrida Does to Rousseau."

The three essays on Nietzsche in *Allegories of Reading* appear at first glance to clarify the issue once and for all. De Man's explicit topic is figurative language, or rather the idea that language is only figurative. The aim of the essay on *The Birth of Tragedy* is to demonstrate that Nietzsche's logocentrism is both asserted and denied by the text. In a sense, de Man repeats the recent French readings of *The Birth of Tragedy* with a twist. The French Nietzscheans read the early texts in the light of the later ones, and conclude that the scope of Nietzsche's work affirms deconstructive practice. De Man is not satisfied with this approach, however, perhaps because of his training in American New Criticism and its belief in the integrity of the individual work. So he bases his reading on a series of unpublished fragments written contemporaneously with *The Birth of Tragedy*. In de Man's reading the fragments contradict Nietzsche's larger claims and expose the work on tragedy as "an extended rhetorical fiction devoid of authority" (101). But using contemporary fragments to enlarge the scope of a work has been made unnecessary by the poststructuralist theory of intertextuality, which sees all texts as subsets of a body of writing. The apparent reason for contradicting the notion of intertextuality in this case would be to strengthen the vision of the work's autonomy, an autonomy traditionally associated, at least in the New Criticism, with the denial of authorial intention. De Man's late reading of Nietzsche would thus stand as an explicit correction of his early essay; it asserts that the ironies and paradoxes of language, not the distance between rhetoric and self, define the scope of human understanding.

In "Literary History and Literary Modernity" the minor term, "rhetoric," already threatens the major term, "Nietzsche." In the *Allegories of Reading* rhetoric subsumes the idea of the self. But as de Man's argument progresses, the repressed "self" struggles to return, and this, we will see, is the key to its power. Both the "Rhetoric of Tropes" and the "Rhetoric of Persuasion" examine the intentional link between selfhood and action in the context of language. The first exposes the phenomenology of consciousness as a metaphysical concept dependent on the persistent error of language. The second reduces the criticism of metaphysics itself to a rhetorical construct. In both chapters, however, de Man discovers in literature the truth of persistent error, although literature is no less deceitful than philosophy simply "because it asserts its own deceitful properties" (115). And the truth of literature leads de Man inevitably to the truth of human relationships. He finds the correspondence in the much-cited "On Truth and Lie in an Extra-Moral Sense," the essay at the heart of the poststructuralist view of Nietzsche: "What is truth? A moving army of metaphors, metonymies and anthropomorphisms, in short a summa of human relationships that are being poetically and rhetorically sublimated . . ." (110).

De Man's reading of "On Truth and Lie" asserts that the idea of the human subject as a "privileged viewpoint" represents the metaphor by which "man protects himself from his insignificance by forcing his own interpretation of the world upon the entire universe, substituting a human-centered set of meanings that is reassuring to his vanity for a set of meanings that reduces him to being a mere transitory accident in the cosmic order" (111). The nature of rhetoric, or language, and not the self, makes the substitution possible, indeed makes avoiding the substitution impossible in de Man's mind. As the substitutions take place, however, another exchange begins to occur in de Man's argument. The more he seems to argue for the rhetoric of tropes, the more the self becomes that rhetoric, and the primacy of language in the action of substitution is replaced by the primacy of the self. "The metaphorical substitution," de Man explains, "is aberrant but no human self could come into being without error" (111). In short, human intelligence only exists in a world of error: the world of error is the world of human consciousness. De Man continues:

> The attributes of centrality and of selfhood are being exchanged in the medium of language. Making the language that denies the self into a center rescues the self linguistically at the same time that it asserts its insignificance, its emptiness as a mere figure of speech. It can only persist as self if it is displaced into the text that denies it. . . . The deconstruction of the self as metaphor does not end in the rigorous separation of the two categories (self and figure) from each other but ends instead in an exchange of properties that allows for their mutual persistance [sic] at the expense of literal truth. . . . By calling the subject a text, the text calls itself, to some extent, a subject. (111–12)

In de Man's early essay, Nietzsche was the subject whose alienation from knowledge was expressed in his rhetoric. In the late essays, the individual subject is no longer held responsible for the persistence of error, but subjectivity has not disappeared. A new subjectivity emerges, and it possesses greater strength and a broader grasp because it is allied with the power of language. The self is more insistent than ever, for language has become the force through which subjectivity represents its errors. One is tempted to say that language has been anthropomorphized. The rhetoric of linguistic substitution merely reflects the unending reiteration of human error, a generalized application of what Freud refers to in *Beyond the Pleasure Principle* as the passive form of the repetition-compulsion, in which a flaw in individual personality compels one to repeat the same experiences as if pursued by a malignant fate. Such is the fate as well of all subjects, especially artists and philosophers, in de Man's eyes. It is especially illuminating in this regard that de Man never wrote on Freud.[4] De

---

[4] See Richard Klein, "The Blindness of Hyperboles: The Ellipses of Insight," *Diacritics* 3, no. 2 (1973): 33–44. In a late interview de Man indicated that Heidegger plays the role for him that Freud plays for Derrida in the deconstructive enterprise. It should be noted, however, that Freud does not figure significantly in Heidegger's work. Consequently,

Man's view of the self derives great force from psychoanalysis, and his reliance on Freud's ideas grows apparent when seen in the light of the work done by Lacan on the language of the self. The allegory of error in de Man is the self, and the self provides philosophy with its strongest model. "If we read Nietzsche," de Man concludes, "with the rhetorical awareness provided by his own theory of rhetoric we find that the general structure of his work resembles the endlessly repeated gesture of the artist 'who does not learn from experience and always again falls into the same trap.' What seems to be most difficult to admit is that this allegory of errors is the very model of philosophical rigor" (118). In other words, language produces a series of rhetorical substitutions that translate what are usually thought of as the self's errors into philosophical rigor and power. The self wins power by embracing itself as error.

As de Man's work evolves, he seeks more and more to rebut the traditional idea that Nietzsche's career embodies a progressive and intentional shift from problems of rhetoric to questions of the self. What de Man's readings demonstrate, however, is his own inability to move within language away from the self, in effect, reproducing the Freudian view that linguistic play performs the unconscious motivations of subjectivity. The final expression of the problem occurs in *The Rhetoric of Romanticism* with "Anthropomorphism and Trope in the Lyric," de Man's last and uncompleted attempt to formulate the interference between selfhood and rhetoric.[5] The title itself works as a summary of de Man's concerns, for "anthropomorphism" acts as a cipher for the process of reading that achieves understanding by representing the play of "trope" or rhetoric as a metaphor of the self. "Anthropomorphism" in de Man's eyes remains the "privileged view-

---

the use of Heidegger merely contributes to de Man's puzzling avoidance of psychoanalysis. I take up this avoidance below as symptomatic of de Man's politics. See Robert Moynihan, "Interview with Paul de Man," *Yale Review* 73, no. 4 (1984): 576–602.

[5] References are to Paul de Man, "Anthropomorphism and Trope in the Lyric," in his *The Rhetoric of Romanticism* (New York: Columbia University Press, 1984), 239–62. De Man wrote this essay especially for the volume, but he died before it received final correction.

point" that saves human beings from insignificance by forcing their interpretations upon the world.

Not surprisingly, the essay begins by citing Nietzsche's definition of truth from "On Truth and Lie," but its actual goal is to trace the relation between anthropomorphism and trope (or self and rhetoric) in two poems by Baudelaire. Nietzsche's point remains that human understanding occurs by passing from language to consciousness via anthropomorphism, and de Man finds the same displacement in Baudelaire's "Correspondances" and "Obsession."[6] The earlier "Correspondances" contains no overtly anthropomorphic tendencies; and yet according to de Man it is incomprehensible unless one reads it anthropomorphically. The poem pivots on the pure power of affirmation found in its declarative sentences: "La Nature est un temple," "Il est des parfums." The critical tradition, however, wishes to realize the ideal of "correspondances" by granting to the poetic "comme" the power of transport and by magically uniting man and nature in the "forêts de symboles." De Man offers his own anthropomorphic reading in which the poem's "vivant piliers" metamorphose into the rigid figures of a Paul Delvaux painting, and its "transports de l'esprit" recall the right of transfer, or "correspondance," of the Paris métro. De Man does not escape the tradition of the poem's reading with his interpretation, for he continues to privilege an anthropomorphic rhetoric. Nevertheless, he constantly stresses the obstacles placed by the poem in the way of such a reading. The most forceful example is Baudelaire's use of "comme" in the second half of the poem. De Man argues that the word no longer offers the unity of simile but becomes a grammatical device for enumeration. The poem collapses into a list rather than transporting the reader into a world of glorious totality and unity. The lyric song of "Qui chantent les transports de l'esprit et des sens" becomes the stutter of enumeration: "comme les hautbois," "comme les prairies," and "comme l'ambre." The aim of "Correspondances" is defeated by the very nature of metaphor (*metaphorein*), which as the vehicle of correspondence refuses to transport anything.

[6]References are to Charles Baudelaire, "Correspondances" and "Obsession," in *Oeuvres complètes,* 2 vols. (Paris: Gallimard, 1974), 1:11 and 1:73, respectively.

"Correspondances" thus exemplifies de Man's theory of rhetoric, for the poem's language refers only to itself and refuses to convey any meaning beyond the serenity of its own diction. The poem lays "stress on language as the stage of disjunction" (245). At every point, by way of its very substitutions, it disrupts "the chain of tropological substitution" necessary to unite "aesthetics with epistemology" (250). As de Man explains it, "within the confines of a system of transportation— or of language as a system of communication—one can transfer from one vehicle to another, but one cannot transfer from being like a vehicle to being like a temple, or a ground" (252). De Man means that rhetoric refuses to establish a correspondence between meaning and being; rather, its meanings rely on a series of substitutions and displacements equal in signification and isolation from any ground in reality. Truth, in the Nietzschean sense, is only an "army of metaphors," and it acts to expose the power of language to create an illusion of reality by advancing from meaning to meaning.

After such a reading of "Correspondances," it hardly seems necessary that de Man turn to "Obsession." He has already accomplished with the first poem all that his theory of rhetoric promises. He has traced the desire to represent human consciousness and its frustration by language, claiming that desire can persist only by representing itself through the language that denies it; indeed, he has suggested that the desire itself is rhetorical. But the obsessive nature of this desire needs illustration, and Baudelaire's poem provides de Man with a spectacular instance of the terrors of anthropomorphism. "Obsession" depicts a nightmarish world in which every object emits a human cry of despair: "ce rire amer / De l'homme vaincu, plein de sanglots et d'insultes, / Je l'entends dans le rire énorme de la mer." It demonstrates the desire of human beings to extend their power beyond themselves by anthropomorphizing the world.

According to de Man, "Correspondances" and "Obsession" are mirror images of one another. "Obsession" is lyric, de Man's explains, unlike "Correspondances," which exposes the limits of the lyric. Whereas "Correspondances" makes impossible the union of aesthetics and epistemology and refuses recuperation in terms of "metaphors of the self," "Obsession" carries out the union of aesthetics and epistemology by representing metaphors of the self as a form of self-consciousness. Indeed, "Obsession" is vividly self-conscious, so much so that it risks twisting the self-consciousness of knowledge into the narcissism of madness. "Obsession" parodies the wish for the correspondences of knowledge by offering a view in which everything swims together in madness and horror. Its vision of enlightenment is expressly fitted for de Man's theory of blindness and insight, for the moment of illumination comes with the blindness of anthropomorphism, when light speaks its language: "la lumière parle un langage connu."

"Correspondances" makes no sense unless it is read anthropomorphically, and "Obsession" reads itself and "Correspondances" in that manner. Indeed, reading is anthropomorphic. The bottom line remains that any reading of "Correspondances" (or any poem) becomes a writing of "Obsession." The defensive motion of understanding, described by Nietzsche, transforms language into self, advances from the truth of rhetoric to that of anthropomorphism, and crystallizes in the obsessive desire for power.

Despite the apparent differences between "Correspondances" and "Obsession," however, de Man ultimately fails to oppose them. The theoretical and tenuous distinction with which he proposes to separate the two poems hangs on the radical hypothesis that there could be such a thing as "pure rhetoric." One could define the idea of pure rhetoric as the possibility that meaning could be other than a human product. It is the ultimate creation of philosophical skepticism because it conceives of the meanings with which human beings must live as alien to those same human beings. It is the logical opposite of anthropomorphism because it denies that human beings possess the power to create meaning. Meaning becomes, by definition, a position in language that human beings cannot control while retaining their humanity. Thus de Man imagines "Correspondances" as the "flat surface of time" to which the elegiac mourning of "Obsession" adds human remembrance. In short, language is inhuman; it appears to be about the absence of the self. This hypothesis might be mistaken for the classic problem of representing nothingness, of asking whether nothing *is*, but if de Man has taught us anything, it has been that literature is not in the slightest interested in nothingness as a phenomenon but only in forms of error and knowledge, that is, in blindness and insight. De Man's theory of rhetoric is, rather, a working out of the skeptical desire to rid the self of its blindness in order to attain a vision of meaning pure and unsullied by human error, in sum, a vision of perfect intellectual power. Words such as "blindness" and "insight," even if used to describe language's relation to itself, find their greatest power only in relation to the self.

Pure rhetoric can exist only in the absence of the self, and since the writing and reading selves cannot or will not posit their own absence, pure rhetoric is only a theory. De Man's originality consists in his willingness to conceive of this theory. The effort has attracted him to the great madmen of Western literature, to Rousseau, Nietzsche, and Baudelaire, and to figures of premature death such as Keats and Shelley. In each case, de Man demonstrates how faith in rhetoric betrays the desire for progress in civilization and permanence in life, and the defaced corpse of the author becomes an inseparable part of his work. In "Shelley Disfigured," de Man concludes that Shelley's *Triumph of Life* exposes the arbitrariness of language, and he enshrines the poet's disfigured body as the symbol of this deadly arbitrariness personified. Similarly, in "Autobiography as De-Facement," de Man describes autobiography as a rhetoric that strives to restore life to its subject, but autobiographic rhetoric ends by restoring only the disfigurement of death, a death mask, or what he calls a "displaced name for a linguistic predicament" (81).[7]

A theory of pure rhetoric would indeed require that death assume the form of a linguistic predicament, but the ultimate test of any rhetoric, as de Man explains in "Shelley Disfigured," depends on how one disposes of the body. And de Man has not been able to dispose of the body. Whenever he attempts to eliminate the constitutive self of rhetoric, he ends by writing about its death. In the end, de Man's theory is not a theory of rhetorical reading at all but a theory of mourning, like Baudelaire's "Obsession" and its "Chambres d'éternel deuil où vibrent de vieux râles," in which the anguished and skeptical self, obsessed

[7]Paul de Man, "Autobiography as De-Facement," and "Shelley Disfigured," in his *The Rhetoric of Romanticism*, 67–82, 92–124.

with its own loss, tries again and again to reconstitute itself in the act of mourning. Rhetoric is always a rhetoric of the self; mourning is always a mourning over death and not over absence, despite de Man's aspiration "to allow for non-comprehension and enumerate non-anthropomorphic, non-elegiac, non-celebratory, non-lyrical, non-poetic, that is to say, prosaic, or, better, *historical* modes of language power" (262). De Man's theories drive inexorably to the point where the skeptical insight that rhetoric kills the self fails to be stated in a rhetoric other than that of the self. Just as Nietzsche's definition of truth collapses in anthropomorphism—for truth is an *army* of metaphors—so de Man's obsession with blindness and insight finds truth in theory that language alone can *see*.

Paul de Man died in 1983, but the mourning for him has not ceased. His name continues to appear in various dedications and expressions of regret. The special issue of *Yale French Studies* on "The Lesson of Paul de Man" reads like an elegy.[8] The funeral orations printed in the issue chart each speaker's first or most personal experience with Paul de Man, and they tell, inevitably, of death; or, rather, they tell of Paul de Man engaged in an act of reading inseparable from the act of mourning. Each scene pictures de Man reading a text about death: Peter Brooks remembers de Man reading Yeats's "At Algeciras—A Meditation on Death"; Geoffrey Hartman cites de Man's fascination with the "cold mortality" of Shelley; and Jacques Derrida repeats de Man's reading of Mallarmé's "Tombeau de Verlaine" and exposes his own feelings of "la mort dans l'âme." Surely, the occasion of the orations has something to do with these memories: people look for talk about death in the event of death. But I want to explore the possibility that the funeral orations were true to de Man's method of reading: reading in de Man's definition always exposes a rhetoric of selfhood, in which the skeptical self first negates itself and then seizes power by mourning its own loss.

Mourning implies a fusion of identities, and thus, a confusion over identity. But what happens in the event of a double mourning? Given the fusion of identity characteristic of mourning, can such a thing as a

[8] *Yale French Studies* 69 (1985).

double mourning take place? What would it mean to have one's mourning interrupted by mourning?

A process of mourning has interrupted another mourning. The victims of the Holocaust are now mourned in the same place as some mourn for Paul de Man. De Man's youthful anti-Semitism has created a structural interference between his own death and the death of six million Jews. The effect is a loss of mourning, a loss of the loss, that is baffling, embarrassing, and pernicious. It is baffling because the figure of de Man has become a symbol for his own mourning as well as for the mourning of the Jews. It is embarrassing because the discovery of de Man's collaborationist writings proves a scandal to every critic who has at one time or another admired his work, and this scandal has become the basis of attacks on critical theory itself. It is pernicious, potentially, because the confusion of identities in mourning has transformed de Man into a martyr figure whose insistence makes it more difficult to concentrate on the Jewish victims of the Holocaust. In this last case, one hears an implicit defense of de Man, suggesting that the theory, the man, or the career are the victims of a youthful anti-Semitism. While many people have refused to defend de Man, quite a few feel sorry for him. This form of regret represents de Man as his own victim or as a victim of anti-Semitism and obstructs our view of the real victims. We mourn de Man as "Jew" instead of the Jews.[9] What are the consequences of this kind of reading for de Man's relation to the victims of the Holocaust? How do these consequences figure in the mourning of Paul de Man?

[9] The natural evolution of this tendency is to see de Man as a "Jewish" victim. Richard Rand actually makes this claim, calling de Man's writings a threat because they are "Jewish." See Richard Rand, *"Rigor Vitae,"* in *Responses: On Paul de Man's Wartime Journalism,* ed. Werner Hamacher, Neil Hertz, and Thomas Keenan (Lincoln: University of Nebraska Press, 1989), 350–55.

Jean-François Lyotard, in *Heidegger and "the jews,"* trans. Andreas Michel and Mark Roberts (Minneapolis: University of Minnesota Press, 1990), makes a similar argument in the context of the Heidegger affair: he invents a category called "the jews," which is fundamental to exclusionary behavior but prior to the existence of the historical persecution of the Jewish people. This category allows him to talk about the exclusion of "the jews" rather than about the politics of anti-Semitism and the Holocaust, a repulsive tactic considering that his topic is Heidegger's relation to national socialism. For a brief analysis of the Heidegger affair, see chapter 7.

There can be only a personal response to these questions. For, inevitably, the questions lead to an argument ad hominem. By "ad hominem," I do not mean, necessarily, that we must interrogate the person of Paul de Man to understand his method of reading. This has already occurred and will no doubt continue, but the facts are simply too clear in what is most important to bear a "reading" in the de Manian sense, which explains why those who have tried to defend him through rhetorical readings (Derrida and Shoshana Felman, for example) have decidedly failed.[10] There exists an early essay entitled "Les Juifs dans la littérature actuelle," in which de Man makes his anti-Semitism evident for all to see.[11] At this level, the immediate and popular response—the *New York Times* response—is correct and truthful. Any attempt to invalidate this response, to turn it aside as too popular, for example, will reproduce an elitism as virulent as de Man's youthful prejudice. The popular response is more important than ever in this case because its very existence stands as a challenge to elitism and because it provides the opportunity to place the university in dialogue with the politics of the everyday world.[12]

Rather, by "ad hominem," I refer to the process of introjection or

[10] Both Derrida and Felman build their defenses on the essentially de Manian superadded technique of New Critical close reading in order to highlight the kinds of paradoxes and ironies in de Man's wartime writings that might serve to place in doubt his commitment to nazism. But in this age of skepticism no one can read these extended feats of interpretation with any kind of belief; nor should they. See Derrida's "Like the Sound of the Sea Deep Within a Shell: Paul de Man's War," in the *Responses* volume 127–64, and Shoshana Felman, "Paul de Man's Silence," *Critical Inquiry* 15, no. 4 (1989): 704–44.

[11] Paul de Man, "Les Juifs dans la littérature actuelle," *Le Soir* 55, no. 4 (4 March 1941): 10. De Man's complete writings of the period, more or less, are reproduced in Paul de Man, *Wartime Journalism, 1939–1943,* ed. Werner Harmacher, Neil Hertz, and Thomas Keenan (Lincoln: University of Nebraska Press, 1988).

[12] Early assessments in the press include: Geoffrey Hartman's "Blindness and Insight: Paul de Man, Fascism, and Deconstruction," *New Republic,* 7 March 1988, 26–33; Walter Kendrick, "Blindness and Hindsight: Dispatches from the de Man Front," *Village Voice Literary Supplement,* October 1988; David Lehman, "Deconstructing de Man's Life," *Newsweek,* 15 February 1988, 63; and Jon Wiener, "Deconstructing de Man," *Nation,* 9 January 1988, 22–24. The last two were heavily attacked by academia for errors. Lehman's article is especially disturbing because its layout, which juxtaposes pictures of de Man and Nazi soldiers on the march, bears a remarkable similarity to the original page of *Le Soir* where de Man's essay first appeared in that both use excessive images to implicate the accused and to fascinate their audience. Lehman's book, *Signs of the Times: Deconstruction and the Fall of Paul de Man* (New York: Poseidon Press,

incorporation found in mourning. In mourning, a body is incorporated in the mourner, so that the figure of the absent one becomes a constant trope within the mourner's attempts to read the world. The reaction to Paul de Man's death produced this kind of iconography, and present Holocaust studies continue to grapple with the problem of mourning in similar terms, returning again and again to the iconography of the death camps to stage inhuman memories.

Mourning insists on giving body to the language of the dead. De Man's skeptical theory of reading, of course, claims that a structural interference exists between anthropomorphism and trope. When we read tropes, according to this theory, we always read anthropomorphically, thereby misreading language. De Man's originality consisted in his rigorous attempts to read against the grain of anthropomorphism in order to discover language in itself; he struggled to describe language as a value that exceeds human understanding and that human beings seek to humanize as a result. But by the logic of his own argument, his reading must necessarily collapse into human terms. Here is a double movement, in which each phase is indicative of mourning. Mourning tries to incorporate into human terms a figure colored by death, and de Man's attempt to read "inhumanly," to paraphrase his description of language, strives to undo mourning's originary impulse in order to be done with mourning before its activity accomplishes its own end.[13]

If it seems that I am overemphasizing the relation between reading and mourning in de Man's work, we might recall that "Anthropomor-

---

1991), lamely defends the *Newsweek* article, by stretching the truth about its format, describing it as occupying three pages instead of one, and arguing that critics have focused on the format of the essay rather than its content because they have no other choice (215). A response from academia to the de Man affair may be found in Werner Hamacher, Neil Hertz, and Thomas Keenan, eds., *Responses: On Paul de Man's Wartime Journalism* and in *Critical Inquiry* 15, no. 4 (1989), an issue devoted to the scandal. I also recommend Reed Way Dasenbrock, "Paul de Man, the Modernist as Fascist," *South Central Review* 6 (Summer 1989): 6–18, who argues that de Man's fascism should be seen in the context of the intellectual variety espoused by Pound and others during the same period.

[13] The term "inhuman" arises in a discussion of de Man's "Task of the Translator," in his *The Resistance to Theory* (Minneapolis: University of Minnesota Press, 1986), 94–99.

phism and Trope in the Lyric," one of his last essays, defines reading specifically in the context of mourning. This is not a limited context but one that applies to all reading. De Man claims that a kind of double textuality, a competition between two senses, exists in every reading. This double textuality, as we saw earlier, can be briefly summarized in the relation between Baudelaire's two poems "Correspondances" and "Obsession": "There always are at least two texts, regardless of whether they are actually written out or not; the relationship between the two sonnets . . . is an inherent characteristic of any text" (260–61). The relationship between the two sonnets consists of the play between a nonhuman, purely linguistic world of enumeration and a psychological obsession with reading this world in anthropomorphic terms, the paradox of de Man's theory being that the obsessive reading is not the product of a human psychology but its creation in language. The essay ends by trying to capture true mourning in a description of pure reading, so that true mourning and rhetorical reading merge into a single act: "If mourning is called a 'chambre d'éternel deuil où vibrent de vieux râles,' then this pathos of terror states in fact the desired consciousness of eternity and of temporal harmony as voice and as song. True 'mourning' is less deluded. The most *it* can do is to allow for non-comprehension and enumerate non-anthropomorphic, non-elegiac, non-celebratory, non-lyrical, non-poetic, that is to say, prosaic, or, better, *historical* modes of language power" (262; de Man's emphases). "True mourning" is emphatically an *"it"* because it does not stabilize itself around the figure of a human being, thereby creating an aesthetic or ethical object. In other words, it reads its history purely as language power. But this effect is in fact closer to melancholy than to mourning. For melancholy is the activity of mourning for an object that cannot be either objectified or incorporated at a conscious level. In other words, when de Man attempts to purify mourning of its object, he finds not true mourning but true melancholy.

I have always felt that de Man's writings evoked a sense of melancholy. Some critics have accused him of nihilism, but they have confused the nothingness of nihilism with the repression of the human object found in melancholy. The discovery of de Man's collaborationist writings finally provides a motivation for his melancholic refusal of the object of mourning. Melancholy allows the mourning of the loss of a loss; and politically, in terms of de Man's past, it describes an activity of mourning in which the object of mourning, the Jews, cannot be named.

This effect becomes strongest and most apparent with the death of de Man himself because the response of his disciples both amplifies and exposes it. De Man's theory of reading asks us to interpret without constituting a human object, and a whole generation of his students reads in this manner. Yet when they confront the death of Paul de Man, their reading breaks down, as he predicted reading always must, because their interpretations fix on the figure of the charismatic and smiling mentor.[14] But this imperative to mourn for de Man gains extra purchase when we realize that a subtext exists in which he is already performing a reading that wills to mourn without a human object but fails because this reading always turns back on itself, egotistically, to constitute the reader—in this case, Paul de Man—as the object of mourning. To name the objects, de Man's reading tries not to mourn for the Jews in his past, but it turns necessarily into a mourning for his own past. The sorrow of the Jews becomes an opportunity for inventing his own critical power. Here one would have to trace how "history" in de Man's theory works specifically as a metaphor for the violent history of World War II. One would also have to expose de Man's use of a rhetoric of marginality as well as his talent for appropriating the victimhood of authors such as Rousseau, Hölderlin, Shel-

---

[14] The iconography attending de Man's death has been overwhelming. "The Lesson of Paul de Man," the volume of *Yale French Studies* (69 [1985]) dedicated to his work and published upon his death, places a portrait of the smiling de Man on the cover. The *Responses* volume begins with a full portrait, as if it were a Festschrift and not an assessment of collaborationist writings, but here de Man is frowning slightly. The advertisements for this volume and for the collection of wartime journalism by the University of Nebraska Press used a floating mask on which parts of de Man's features had been superimposed. Finally, the poster for a conference on the wartime journalism, held in Belgium, used a portrait of de Man as a child, as if the person to be discussed at the conference was frozed forever at this stage of development. Jerome Christensen has discussed the iconography of critical theory and some of its uses in the de Man controversy in "From Rhetoric to Corporate Populism: A Romantic Critique of the Academy in an Age of High Gossip," *Critical Inquiry* 16, no. 2 (1990): 438–65.

ley, Keats, Baudelaire, Nietzsche, and Rilke.[15] The surprise is that de Man's disciples cannot imitate his reading because a true reading in this style would always name the reader as the mourned object, but his students turn to discipleship instead, that is, they name de Man in place of themselves.

It would take considerable space to justify this hypothesis, but let me turn briefly to two cases to suggest what shape the argument might take. The first case is de Man's relation to Freud, which has been difficult for critics to pin down. He seems at times to use a Freudian discourse, but he rarely names Freud. Richard Klein has tried to trace the association, and he expresses amazement at the fact that de Man manages to maneuver without ever referring to Freud. Yet Klein does not resituate Freud in de Man's text. More recently, Cynthia Chase has written about de Man's relation to Freud in terms of the idea of resistance, but she does so without naming the most obvious point of attachment.[16] De Man's "Resistance to Theory" echoes Freud's "Resistances to Psycho-Analysis" on many fronts, the most interesting one in this context being a parallel between Freud's solitary stand against anti-Semitism and de Man's solitary stand against the Modern Language Association. Of course, de Man also repeats Freud's argument that resistance to psychoanalysis demonstrates the truth of psychoanalysis, concluding that the resistance to theory is theory itself. But for Chase resistance is not really a Freudian concept; it becomes de Man's word. Playing the good disciple, she suppresses Freud's influence in her mentor's text and makes de Man even more de Manian.

I cannot help thinking in this context of the article "Une Doctrine juive: Le Freudisme," printed next to de Man's text of anti-Semitism in *Le Soir*. Here is a true phantom text, close to de Man's, bordering on it, and yet not the same text. Its author contends that Freud's own disciples made his theory more Jewish than it was, giving it additional force in a "société décadente et enjuivée [decadent and Judaized soci-

[15] See the chapter "Paul de Man and the Triumph of Falling," in my book *The Ethics of Criticism* (Ithaca, N.Y.: Cornell University Press, 1988), 98–123.

[16] Cynthia Chase, "The Witty Butcher's Wife: Freud, Lacan, and the Conversion of Resistance to Theory," *MLN* 102, no. 5 (1987): 989–1013.

ety]." Similarly, de Man's "Les Juifs dans la littérature actuelle" strives to save modern literary phenomena from an apparent decadence, "parce que enjuivés [because Judaized]," by describing their ability to purify themselves of Jewish influences. The irony, according to de Man, remains that "vulgar anti-Semitism" views modern literature as decadent because it fails to comprehend the essentially anti-Semitic nature of modern (Jewish) forms! This explains, incidentally, why the name of Kafka, sometimes invoked in de Man's wartime journalism, does not translate into a subtle resistance to Nazi anti-Semitism.

In the specific case of Freud, then, we try to name Freud as Jew in de Man's text, but we end by naming instead a textuality that will not permit his Jewishness to emerge. We discover, in short, a textuality whose essence is a Jewish refusal of Jewishness, a textuality whose force resembles all too clearly the aporias described in the theories of Paul de Man.

The second case is de Man's relation to Derrida. I want to suggest, half seriously, that Derrida has become de Man's disciple. There have always been those who have tried to name de Man as a disciple of Derrida, but the label has not held. Others have tried to purify Derrida of the "vulgar Americanism" of de Manian deconstruction, but Derrida has himself rendered the attempt ineffective by turning to de Man for guidance, and his critical purpose has noticeably slackened in the wake of the de Man affair. The initial encounter between Derrida and de Man occurs in "The Rhetoric of Blindness," where de Man outmaneuvers Derrida at his own game by giving away the game to Rousseau. Derrida is the master of the skeptical game, "Whoever loses wins," but de Man underbids Derrida in a kind of intellectual equivalent to golf by coming in with a lower score.[17] Derrida deconstructs Rousseau, but de Man names Rousseau as the exemplary case of self-indictment on which the text of modern philosophy is founded. Rousseau deconstructs himself, de Man argues, and Derrida is guilty of trying to win, simply because he takes Rousseau as an object. Reading without this object, in a minor key, as it were, de Man transforms all

[17] Derrida locks on to the phrase "Whoever loses wins," in his *Margins of Philosophy*, trans. Alan Bass (Chicago: University of Chicago Press, 1982), 20.

textuality into that of "Rousseau." By losing himself to Rousseau, de Man wins the right to be "Rousseau."[18]

Derrida is still reeling from his initial encounter with de Man. He dedicates books to de Man, as if he were the disciple. He returns to the scene to replay the debate. Whether Derrida's gesture bespeaks true admiration or only makes the attempt to underbid the master in order to make him "win" is probably unimportant. For both gestures belong to the same game. The point is moot in the end because de Man died prematurely, making it difficult to underbid him. Derrida then turned to the lecture circuit, reading his private correspondence with de Man on stage. He has appointed himself de Man's chief defender in the United States. He wrote *Mémoires* for his departed friend, while simultaneously trying to write his own life story.[19]

Mémoires is, above all, a work of mourning, but it is less obvious that it also imitates de Man's method of reading. Derrida creates two powerful and personal analogies that rely ultimately on de Man's technique in "The Rhetoric of Blindness." First, he accepts de Man's description of Hölderlin's "sacred singularity" and then gives that position to de Man, the "Hölderlin in America." Second, Derrida repeats de Man's reading of Rousseau for de Man: "Always already, as Paul de Man says, there is deconstruction at work in the work of Rousseau. . . . Always already, there is deconstruction at work in the work of Paul de Man . . ." (124). *Mémoires* shows that Derrida has learned the proper humility from de Man. He will not attempt an act of mastery this time. He will win only by giving in to loss. Indeed, *Mémoires* plays out a strange transference, in which Derrida appropriates de Man's funereal marginality by giving everything away to him. The book situates de Man amid the constellation of the great mad and

[18] In chapter 2 we saw an equivalent of this process in the dynamics of charisma. Indeed, de Man produced his personal charisma on the basis of this maneuver, appropriating the power of past masters by giving away his power to them. This further explains why the attempts on the part of de Man's disciples to duplicate this maneuver fail. They are not able to give away their critical power, and they end by reincorporating it in the figure of the charismatic teacher.

[19] References are to Jacques Derrida, *Mémoires: For Paul de Man,* trans. Cecile Lindsay, Jonathan Culler, and Eduardo Cadava (New York: Columbia University Press, 1986).

charismatic thinkers of Western modernity but remains oddly silent about its author. De Man, not Derrida, is responsible for "deconstruction in America." De Man, not Derrida, is the object of attacks. Derrida does not speak in his own name. "Il donne au nom de l'autre."

To give to the name of the other, or to give in the name of the other, serves the work of mourning. But it also plays the game between reading and mourning discovered by Paul de Man. This game secretly guided the relationship between Derrida and de Man for many years, but it could no longer be contained when de Man died. When Derrida spoke at de Man's funeral of "la mort dans l'âme," he finally presented the problem of mourning as introjection in explicit terms, although it had been there implicitly for a long time. In short, Derrida encounters de Man's melancholy, his relentless desire to read without an object other than himself, and like the good student, like de Man himself (for de Man is his own best student), he turns it into mourning by naming the master as object.

How de Man's disciples react to the wartime journalism will be interesting, to say the least. For now de Man has really lost the game. His situation is closest to that of the mature Nietzsche, another master of the skeptical game of winning by losing. After a lifetime of trying to find a position of marginality and uniqueness, Nietzsche attained the position posthumously when his sister gave him away to the Nazis, thus transforming him into a convenient icon for everything that the West has now rejected. The future of de Man's theories depends on whether the present "loss" can be construed as a "win" and on whether his followers can continue to name their master as an object. If they are able to name de Man in their texts, the work of mourning and anthropomorphism will continue. If they cannot name de Man, if they refuse the object, their writings risk turning melancholic. In both cases, however, whether they name or repress de Man, their readings may well continue to repeat a melancholy subtext that refuses to name the true object of mourning.

If reading and mourning are indeed parallel structures, as de Man's theory suggests, then there is no way out of this dilemma, and we are destined to remember or to repress the figure of de Man in the space that he left open for that purpose. But if this parallel is merely an effect of de Man's personal and political history, then we should be aware of the ideological and egotistical intent lurking in any theory that would confuse mourning and reading. De Man's essay on "Les Juifs" concludes with an unmournful solution. He argues that the loss of the Jews will not affect the future of literature:

> En plus, on voit donc qu'une solution du problème juif qui viserait à la création d'une colonie juive isolée de l'Europe, n'entraînerait pas, pour la vie littéraire de l'Occident, de conséquences déplorables. Celle-ci perdrait, en tout et pour tout, quelques personnalités de médiocre valeur et continuerait, comme par le passé, à se développer selon ses grandes lois évolutives.

> Moreover, one sees thus that a solution to the Jewish problem that would lead to the creation of a Jewish colony isolated from Europe would not have for the literary life of the West regrettable consequences. It would lose, all in all, some personalities of mediocre value and would continue, as in the past, to develop according to its higher evolutionary laws.

No doubt, de Man spent the rest of his life mourning this "solution," but he never named the true object of mourning.

If the inevitable outcome of mourning is the incorporation of a figure, let us be sure to remember the right one. The number is six million. Their name in history is the Jews.

5

The Politics of the Politics
of Interpretation

It is perhaps an oddity of the current theoretical scene that the phrase "the politics of interpretation" does not refer specifically to what happens in the classroom when an interpretation takes place but to a general idea about the types of interests that originate the impulse to interpret. The politics of interpretation is not involved directly with world or national politics, although it does not exactly ignore them, and it has little to say about university politics. Rather, the idea of the politics of interpretation is philosophically and theoretically motivated. It tries to trace the conditions of the political as such. It assumes that all meaning is political, and it makes an effort to describe what happens in general when we interpret. Such generality merely reaffirms the theoretical dimension of the notion, and I will not do it an injustice if I claim that this theory is fairly constant across a broad diversity of schools and camps. The politics of interpretation usually describes the "political" as that realm in which competing interests struggle to gain power. Power drives interpretation, it is argued, and the will to interpret would have no will at all if it did not reach toward the possession of power. To interpret, then, is to engage in an act of empowering oneself, usually at the expense of others. This scenario may seem morally repulsive at first, but it is, cold war theorists declare, a dog eat dog world out there, and it is naive to be too offended by the state of

111

affairs, since it is clear that there is no escape from it. It is wiser, they suggest, to play the game, and develop strategies and tactics of one's own.

"Tactics," "strategies," "maneuvers"—these are the typical words used to describe what literary critics do when they interpret. What does it mean that literary criticism has adopted as a means of identifying its own activity a vocabulary whose nearest relative is military artifice? What does it mean to describe the literary work as if it were a battlefield in which "breaches" and "gaps" in the line are to be confronted with great valor and perseverance? Obviously, we are deep within metaphorics, but, of course, a central tenet of cold war theory is that metaphors create political reality. What does it mean for literary criticism that its metaphors for its own activity parallel the rhetoric of the cold war era?[1]

I want to let this question act as a guide while I consider the relationship between the way that we talk about interpretation and the way that we relate to the immediate situation of being in a classroom. If the politics of interpretation is steeped in the skepticism of cold war rhetoric, it may also import these kinds of relations into the classroom situation. What if the skeptical and theoretical relationships that we have to texts are played out in our interpersonal relationships with our students?

With this question, I have stumbled upon a major aporia, as explicated by Paul de Man, in Mikhail Bakhtin's work on dialogism. In "Dialogue and Dialogism," de Man sets in opposition two meanings of the dialogic.[2] On the one hand, dialogism refers to the practical sphere of ethics and politics where it designs a means to resist modes of

[1] It is difficult these days to find good examples of cold war rhetoric, but the chief of the KGB, Vladimir A. Kryuchkov (since removed during the August coup), has provided one in his argument that the Soviet Union should accept no economic aid from the West: "There are attempts from abroad to exert overt and covert pressure on the Soviet Union and to impose doubtful ideas and plans to pull the country out of a difficult situation. All these efforts often screen a desire to strengthen not so much us, but their own position in our country" (*New York Times,* 23 December, 1990, p. 1. col. 6). My point will be that postwar critical theorists tend to take the same skeptical view of dialogue, cooperation, altruism, and other interpretive relationships crucial to the classroom.

[2] References are to Paul de Man, "Dialogue and Dialogism," in his *The Resistance to Theory* (Minneapolis: University of Minnesota Press, 1986), 106–14.

totalitarian authority. The polyvocal character of the dialogic enacts a mode of conversation used to enhance the solidarity of subgroups and secret communities in repressive societies. Its function is libertarian and revolutionary, and it confronts the univocal nature of authority with a dizzying playfulness. De Man glosses this political function by citing Hegel's idea that prose begins in slavery (108). Like the slave, de Man asserts, "Bakhtin's novelist is persecuted per definition and carries within himself the image of liberation" (108). In short, the dialogic becomes a covert representation of community played out in the symbolism of the text: "its multivoicedness or heteroglossia," as de Man explains it, "postulates distinct and antagonistic class structures as well as the celebratory crossing of social barriers" (108). The dialogism of the text thus exemplifies the dialogue necessary to form a revolutionary community.

But de Man does not stop with the analogy between the body of a text and that of a community. He finds a contradictory meaning of the dialogic in Bakhtin's formalistic work. Here, de Man discovers, "it is possible to think of dialogism as a still formal method by which to conquer or to sublate formalism itself. Dialogism is here still a descriptive and metalinguistic term that says something about language rather than about the world" (109). In other words, de Man has uncovered that place where the definition of the dialogical runs into an inescapable impasse. "Dialogism" is a word that contains two contradictory meanings; and while it may look the same whenever we use it, the word oscillates between one meaning and its other. On the one hand, dialogism is an attempt to sustain a radical exteriority beyond formalism by moving from linguistic to social relationships. On the other hand, this dream of exteriority fails because social relationships are never of a dialogic kind: "it is impossible under any conditions or at any time," writes de Man, citing Bakhtin, "to imagine a trope (say, a metaphor) being unfolded into the two exchanges of a dialogue, that is, two meanings parceled out between two separate voices" (111). We may dream of the possibility that dialogism inches its way toward dialogue, de Man insists, but the dialogic is really a formal term for the tendency of language to create an image of multivoicedness, when in fact this image of separate voices, so necessary to dialogue, is merely an

illusion of language and not a vision of community. Texts never pose
questions and answers, or at least not in the way that we imagine them
to occur in conversations. Rather, texts obey a formal principle of
"dialectical imperialism," in which "the hermeneutics of reference are
undecidable" (112). There is no outside or inside of the text that we
could use to symbolize the two positions from which a conversation
takes place; and in the final analysis de Man must conclude that "To
imitate, or to apply Bakhtin, to read him by engaging him in a dialogue, betrays what is most valid in his work" (114).

Whether de Man's reading of Bakhtin is accurate is a matter for
Bakhtinians to dispute. It is no accident, however, that the Bakhtin of
de Man's reading ends up sounding a lot like de Man himself. De Man
made a career of discovering that critical insights are indistinguishable
from their blind spots, and most frequently he illustrated this aporia by
focusing on the undecidability of a theorist's most cherished vocabulary. The implications of de Man's skeptical theory for the politics of
interpretation are not entirely clear, since he avoids direct political
meanings most of the time, but they are fairly clear. The politics of
interpretation, if we follow de Man, is only truly political when it
directs itself not to competing interpretations or to the national, economic, racial, or gender issues found in specific interpretations but to
that tendency in language by which separate positions within language
are falsified. Language consistently lends itself to the misinterpretation
that a startling array of political positions are possible, and we cling to
these positions to define ourselves; but, to use one of de Man's favorite
words, in doing so we fall into "error." The radical positionality of
language is of a kind not to be confused with political positions. There
are no images of political bodies to be read within linguistic structure.

Interpretation is impossible, according to de Man, because it asks us
to choose between two meanings or to translate one meaning into
another meaning, when there is no possibility of there being two meanings. Or, to put it another way, interpretation asks us to move from
one position to another, when only one position is possible. Language
is totalizing and inhuman, de Man reminds us. We cannot have a
conversation with it or in it, and since interpretation involves this

dream of dialogue, it is not only impossible, it is rather "stupid."[3] I use this word not gratuitously but with a precise definition in mind. Elaine Scarry has recently defined "stupidity" as the idea that surges into consciousness when we reduce someone or something to the status of an object. "Stupid" is the name that we use to refer to entities that lack sentience.[4] Interpretation is stupid, for de Man, because it involves the impossible activity of trying to have a conversation with an object. Reading always ends in the impossibility of reading because we cannot find in literary objects the intelligence that we desire to find there.

De Man was one of cold war criticism's most original and inventive theorists, but it was not his skeptical attitude toward literature but the extremes to which he was willing to push this attitude that set him apart. For cold war criticism in general has tried to reduce literature to the status of a thing, first, by insisting on the autonomy of the literary object and, second, by reducing literature to text. De Man cautions us that the temptation to envision an analogy between the nature of textuality and the nature of political bodies is better resisted. Language is about language, he insists, and never about people. But I want to formulate a question precisely in terms of this analogy. What kind of classroom does de Man's theory of interpretation produce? When de Man talks to texts and talks about texts, what are the implications for the way that we talk to and about students? I know that I am anthropomorphizing the text when I say that we might talk to it. But I am going to do it willfully in order to have a conversation with you, not because I am given to anthropomorphism (although I am, and I apologize for it) and not because I hold a nostalgic view of literature (although I do, and I apologize for that too), but because I want to drive home a political point about teaching. I want to insist that the way our theories treat a work of literature mirrors the way that we

---

[3] Hilary Putnam discusses the problem of interpretation's stupidity in "The Craving for Objectivity," in *Realism with a Human Face*, ed. James Conant (Cambridge, Mass.: Harvard University Press, 1990), 120–31, esp. 128–31. I agree with his notion that the present tendency to regard interpretation as a second-class activity reflects a craving for absolutes, that craving absolutes leads to monism, and that monism is a "bad outlook in every area of human life" (131).

[4] Elaine Scarry, *The Body in Pain* (New York: Oxford University Press, 1985).

treat classrooms. I take it that the thing that one must never do in teaching or in a conversation, if one wants to continue teaching and conversing, is to call one's interlocutor stupid.

Never having seen de Man in the classroom, my argument will not be about his teaching practices. I will restrict my argument to the political implications of his theories. Due to recent discoveries about his wartime activities, we know a great deal about his political leanings: his politics began in association with the far right and moved to a more centrist position. But his interpretive metaphors often preserve reactionary associations. Perhaps the best-known example is his discussion of Archie Bunker in "Semiology and Rhetoric," where he begins by opposing the idea of "relevance," expresses Archie Bunker–like frustration with those who cannot read rhetorically, calls Edith Bunker a reader of "sublime simplicity," and goes on to identify Nietzsche and Jacques Derrida as "archie De-bunkers" (9).[5]

On the issue of stupidity, of course, de Man's reading of Edith Bunker is central. Edith is paralleled with the typical interpreter of literature who is interested in justifying the differences between possible meanings of works rather than with de Man who believes that we cannot assert one meaning over another with justification. By calling Edith a reader of "sublime simplicity," de Man in effect uses Archie's name for his wife, "dingbat," to infer that this kind of interpretation is stupid. Elsewhere de Man makes the same inference: he argues that normal interpretation paraphrases certain elements in a text at the expense of others. Interpretation is therefore susceptible to being made to point out consistently what it is trying to conceal. The rhetorical reader knows this about interpretation, but because this kind of interpretation is inevitable, the difference between the hermeneutics of rhetorical readers and of mainstream critics, "who presumably," de Man says, "write paraphrases without worrying about it," is not very great, except with regard to the self-consciousness of the reader. For once we know how interpretation works, de Man writes, "we cannot go back to our original innocence, for one has to be quite smart in order to

[5] References are to Paul de Man's *Allegories of Reading* (New Haven, Conn.: Yale University Press, 1979). See my discussion of skeptical criticism and of "All of the Family" in chapter 1.

pretend convincingly to be dumb" (xii).[6] In short, rhetorical readers insist self-consciously on the fact that they are aware of the inevitable errors in interpretation not so as to improve their interpretations, which cannot be made more accurate through such confessions, but to prove that they are less stupid than the rest of us. Such imperatives duplicate, I have been arguing, the desire of the skeptical self to attain self-mastery by stripping itself of poorer versions of thought.

I must make one more comment about stupidity before I continue. Kant also provided a definition of stupidity. He defined stupidity as the inability to judge. He defined judgment as having a conversation with oneself and others in public. Call it thinking aloud. This is why the liberal tradition puts so much stock in freedom of speech. According to Kant, the denial of freedom of speech actually means the denial of freedom of thought because he believed firmly that one cannot think by oneself.[7] Interpretation, if we follow Kant, is an act of judgment, aesthetic judgment at the very least and political judgment at the most, because it engages us in the act of retelling another's person's story, thereby initiating the dialogue necessary to thinking. To judge is part of interpreting any story—indeed, its most important part—because it begins the work of retelling a story from our own point of view, which means that it brings the story into our life and puts our life into the story. Literature has no life in the absence of judgment. It is stupid without the aid of our intelligence, and when we abandon the right to judge it we are left with little more than the right to be stupid.

I promise to return to stupidity in a moment. In fact, one of my enduring problems is how to avoid it. But, in the meantime, it may be worth considering the work of another literary critic who has invested a great deal in the issue of pedagogy. Jane Tompkins's work is diametrically opposed, I would want to claim, to that of Paul de Man, and it makes a good contrast with which to test my hypothesis about

[6]References are to de Man's foreword to Carol Jacobs, *The Dissimulating Harmony* (Baltimore: Johns Hopkins University Press, 1978), vii–xiii.

[7]I owe this reading of Kant to Hannah Arendt, *Lectures on Kant's Political Philosophy* (Chicago: University of Chicago Press, 1982), and develop it at greater length in chapter 6 and in my *Morals and Stories* (New York: Columbia University Press, 1992), 113–33.

the politics of teaching. Tompkins's criticism is overtly political in terms of specific issues. She does not barricade herself in a theory of literature as monolithic and as towering as that erected by de Man. But this is not to say that she has no theory of literature. *Sensational Designs* elaborates both a theory of canon formation and of the masterpiece in the context of a series of interpretations of noncanonical novels.[8] The interpretations, in flagrant disregard of de Man's theories, attempt to show the specific cultural work in which a novel is engaged by uncovering the political positions important to its era. Tompkins argues that Susan Warner's *Wide, Wide World* attempts to outflank men in power by declaring that it is far more important to conquer one's soul than the world, that Harriet Beecher Stowe's *Uncle Tom's Cabin* places in doubt the hope that slavery could be abolished by the same moral conditions that made it possible, and that Charles Brockden Brown's *Wieland* argues that a progressive liberalization of structures of authority is responsible for the social chaos of its times.

Tompkins's attack on the idea of the masterpiece seems to be equally political. She claims that works do not become masterpieces because they are better than other writings, because they address more universal themes, or because they are more aesthetically pleasing. She argues that politics creates masterpieces. Works of literature are not masterpieces because they have excited diverse and important interpretations or because they possess greater interpretive potential than other works. They excite diverse and important interpretations because they have been positioned by political struggles as the works by which interpretation is to take place. The greater the political power involved, the longer the work is held in the public eye, and the more likely that it will be interpreted again and again, thereby making it increasingly important to an ongoing cultural conversation. Masterpieces are the mediums by which power is symbolized in a political community, and we delude ourselves when we believe that the selection of a masterpiece involves truth or beauty. Rather, the selection of classics is political,

---

[8] References are to Jane Tompkins, *Sensational Designs: The Cultural Work of American Fiction, 1790–1860* (New York: Oxford University Press, 1985). I discuss her work in a different context in my *Ethics of Criticism* (Ithaca, N.Y.: Cornell University Press, 1988), 192–93.

and interpretation of them is the means by which various political parties maintain and struggle toward ascendancy.

Tompkins advances this theory not only to critique the nature of canon formation but to open positions within traditional canons. She is interested in restoring to the canon those works of literature whose place within it, won by popularity in their own day, has been unjustly taken away by the political powers that be. But what does it take to make a noncanonical work canonical? Tompkins's theory tells us. It means to use it to have a conversation about political positions, and to continue to use it in this way for a long time. It means to situate the work within the sphere of interpretation by an act of power. These acts of power are never visible in specific interpretations. Indeed, she argues, interpretation looks so apolitical only because it is the material means by which politics acquires power, and power politics works best when it is conducted in secret.

It looks as if we have returned to the politics of interpretation as usual. Tompkins's description of interpretation looks like it belongs to the skeptical rhetoric of the cold war. We have the usual and obvious mad scramble for power, but it is nevertheless quite difficult to discover the workings of these power plays. They are irresistible, malignant, and covert at the same time. If we ask, as is my project here, what kind of classroom this theory of literature produces, it seems that we are due for a great deal of unpleasantness. Tompkins describes how various aspiring authors—Hawthorne and Brown, for example—sent their books to politicians or involved themselves in their campaigns. In the classroom version of these politics, the interpretations and essays written by students would be offerings set before the Queen, whose favoritism would guarantee the rise to power of some over others. Discussion in the classroom would also serve to curry favor. I have to confess that this scenario looks fairly accurate to me. Some of my experiences in graduate school were only too similar.

But I am not convinced that *Sensational Designs* leads to this scenario because it also follows a practice of reading that leads away from its theoretical apparatus. The skeptical theory is that masterpieces are established by political struggle. It is a possible theory, but Tompkins does not really prove it. This may well be due not to its plausibility, which remains to be tested, but to the degree of difficulty involved in proving any literary theory. Tompkins would have to show how a masterpiece is established politically, apart from form and content, and perhaps how a very popular work is demoted politically, apart from form and content. (Incidentally, she succeeds nicely in the first task with the case of Hawthorne's *Scarlet Letter* but offers no analysis of the second kind.) She would then have to repeat these analyses for many, many cases, so that we would be convinced that she is describing a phenomenon that occurs repeatedly and in a configuration that deserves to be called "political." No doubt this is a worthy task, but I would not wish it on anyone.

But there is a further issue. What would such a demonstration purchase for the theory? Would it do away with literature? Would it do away with interpretation? Would it change how interpretation works? Skeptical theory, it seems to me, is always trying to do away with interpretation at the very least and with literature at the very most. But Tompkins does not appear to be interested in these ends, and we know that her theory has not changed the way that she interprets a work of literature. Her reading of *Uncle Tom's Cabin,* to my mind a brilliant interpretation, is still recognizably an interpretation. It does not differ sufficiently from interpretation as usual for one to conclude, "Here we do not have interpretation as we know it." When Tompkins wishes to show how Hawthorne acquired his place in the canon, she traces his relations to people in power. But when she wishes to place Stowe's novel in his company, she does not repeat this kind of analysis, demonstrating that Stowe had as great a claim to prestige as Hawthorne— maybe more—and that she has therefore written a "masterpiece." Instead, she interprets the novel according to themes and historical issues, quoting long passages and performing close readings of them. Tompkins's theory may be necessary to her practice because it serves to create a space in the canon and sets up the motivation to reread sentimental novels. But the theory does not transform the practice of interpretation.

In other words, Tompkins does not stop interpreting once she discovers that interpretation is not an internally coherent activity but a political one. We might say that she encounters the same breach between theory and practice described by Paul de Man, but instead of describing the breach she jumps it or, rather, she fast-talks, interprets, her way across it.[9] Even though her theory holds that canon formation is based not on the idea of the interpretive depth of works but on the politics and power supporting them, she begins the process of discussing the works, of enlarging them, of cropping them, and of interpreting them. The theory of the masterpiece holds that interpretation will prove that a work is a classic by revealing its universality, wisdom, and timelessness, and Tompkins has wisely shown that this is unsupportable, that interpretation cannot verify a masterpiece because all works become masterpieces in interpretation. But the practical repercussions of this claim are limited. Even though it may be incoherent to argue that masterpieces are proven through interpretation, it is not incoherent to so prove them since, arguably, Tompkins does this when she insists that her noncanonical works are worth interpreting. At this point, her skeptical argument against the idea of the masterpiece loses its purchase, as interpretation comes into its own right. The theory is stupid, but the interpretation is not.

Let me be exceptionally clear. I am not saying that the theories of Jane Tompkins are stupid, but that theories in general tend toward stupidity when they call a halt to interpretation. Such skeptical theories express a desire for difference, sometimes defined as authority, and their hatred of interpretation derives from the desire to rise above the everyday world of politics, in which general solutions do not present themselves as much as we would like, in order to achieve a bird's-eye view of the world from which every idea and term seems distinct and controllable. Theory tends to express its vision in all-or-nothing terms. It likes binary oppositions or, lacking them, aporias because although aporias may hurt the brain, they are at least predictable. When theory

[9] The difference that I am positing between Tompkins and de Man is also sketched by Michel Foucault, "Polemics, Politics, and Problematizations," in *The Foucault Reader*, ed. Paul Rabinow (New York: Pantheon Books, 1984), under the separate headings of "dialogue" and "polemics," where dialogue defines a conversation in which parties respect each other's rights and the history of their statements and polemics refers to an adversarial encounter intent upon injuring one's conversant. Remarkably, Foucault defines these terms by reference to the opposition between a counterculture ethic of dialogue and a cold war ethic of polemics (381–83).

turns to politics, therefore, it wants to claim that everything is political because it wants to leave nothing outside its purview.

The concept of a masterpiece is such a theoretical construction. It argues that one work rises above dumb interpretation to stand as a distinctive statement on all times and circumstances. It claims the totalizing view of universality. That we cannot prove why masterpieces are masterpieces, however, should clue us in to the fact that the idea is purely theoretical. It is impossible to show why a masterpiece is a masterpiece because such proof depends on interpretation, but a masterpiece by definition rises above interpretation. The masterpiece is never where the interpretation is. The same may be said about theories of literature in general. We cannot prove our theories because such proofs should depend on the types of interpretations that issue from them, but theorists, by definition, prefer to hover above interpretation. They cannot stay at ground level long enough to allow interpretation to garner the proofs necessary to validate their theories.

My own theory about theory, of course, obeys this kind of impulse. What kind of distinction would I win for myself if I spent these pages interpreting a poem or a novel? Better to advance a theory or better yet a theory of theory.

Does this mean that Tompkins's theory is worthless? No, that remains to be seen. Does this mean that her interpretation is worthless? No, we already know that it is not worthless because it is an interpretation that brings us into dialogue with the novels. It asserts one interpretation, so that interpretation in general may exist. It is not a stupid interpretation because it does not reduce the work of literature to an object. It is an act of judgment that engages the novels in the art of thinking together aloud. "I see their plots and characters," Tompkins says of sentimental novels, "as providing society with a means of thinking about itself, defining certain aspects of social reality which the authors and their readers shared, dramatizing its conflicts, and recommending solutions" (200).

To begin interpreting a work is to empower it to change things as they are. It is to do it the honor of thinking with it in public. When we place a theory before the work of interpretation, I have suggested, we work to empower ourselves at the expense of the text. When we create

a theory that claims that we cannot converse with the work of literature, we sentence the work to silence and stupidity. The usual response
to the sentimental novel, as Tompkins makes clear, was to call it names
rather than to interpret it. It is no accident that this name was usually
some variation of "stupid" or "dummy." The critical tradition had
decided that it did not want to have a conversation with these novels.
First, it told them that they had nothing intelligent to say and that they
were beneath judgment. Then, it told them to shut up. Lately I have
begun to feel that the critical tradition wants to do the same thing to
literature in general.

Tompkins sought out the sentimental novel and restored intelligence
to it. She has made it possible for us to put our lives into these novels
and to take them into our lives. She has rescued them from stupidity,
and that, after all, is the work of a teacher, isn't it? To teach any work
of literature to a student is in some way to follow this practice. It is to
translate one's description of literature into the politics of the classroom. Let me repeat what Tompkins says about sentimental novels
and their role in thinking: "I see their plots and characters as providing
society with a means of thinking about itself, defining certain aspects
of social reality which the authors and their readers shared, dramatizing its conflicts, and recommending solutions" (200). A classroom run
according to this view strikes me as having a great deal of potential for
dialogue.[10]

By interpreting Tompkins's work in this way, I hope that I have
made myself clear. I am suggesting that although some of its theoretical implications risk making conversation difficult, its practice of interpretation unstrings what usually goes today by the name of the politics
of interpretation. Her practice of interpretation produces a world, to
paraphrase Hegel, in which prose begins in slavery, and it is no coinci-
dence that Harriet Beecher Stowe is important to her. Rebellion begins
in practice, not in theory, with the slaves not the overseers, and inter-

[10] The metaphor of conversation is important to the work of Richard Rorty, *Consequences of Pragmatism* (Minneapolis: University of Minnesota Press, 1982) and *Contingency, Irony, and Solidarity* (Cambridge: Cambridge University Press, 1989). For a
critique, see Frank Lentricchia's "Rorty's Cultural Conversation," *Raritan* 3, no. 1
(1983): 136–41, and my "The Ethics of Anti–Ethnocentrism," *Michigan Quarterly
Review* 32 no. 1 (1993): 41–70.

pretation, that most untheorizable of things, rebels in its practice. I am not sure it would be possible to create a theory about why Stowe's novel was such an astounding success. Such success rebels against theories, especially political theories. Indeed, is not Stowe's novel about the fact that politics is not enough? Stowe, as Tompkins explains it, regarded as superficial, as mere extensions of the worldly policies that produced the slave system, those activities that constitute the most effective political measures for us (132). By being the most unpolitical of novels, *Uncles Tom's Cabin* somehow becomes the most political of novels, and it thereby resists the theory that all interpretations are political in the usual way. This theory is worth resisting because it commits the errors habitual to theory. Such theories of the political want everything to be political, to be wholly and purely political, in order to place everything in their grasp. They want nothing nonpolitical to exist. But this is never how politics works in reality. The wildest dreams of success experienced in the most powerful moments of political ascendancy fall short of this fantasy. Never for an instant has real politics achieved everything that it desires. If *Uncle Tom's Cabin* shows us anything, it is that political power has such limits.

What does this tell us about politics in the classroom? This is a delicate question, and I pose it not because I have any answers but because I want to think about it in public. Politics, it seems to me, enters the classroom in two forms. First, especially in literature departments, it takes the form of what I have been calling the politics of the politics of interpretation. Second, it may take the form of a particular political agenda usually elaborated by the teacher. I find it extremely difficult to express my views on these two forms of politics. On the one hand, the politics of the politics of interpretation, I have been arguing, promotes a politics of nondialogue resembling the skeptical rhetoric of the cold war era. It takes the moral high ground by criticizing politics from such a high altitude that it cannot be said to be political at all. My impulse is to call it cowardly. It poisons the political process by holding it in contempt, and it seeks at the same time to empower itself to the disadvantage of everything else. It is top-heavy, hierarchical, and authoritarian. On the other hand, I recognize the force of skeptical argument to uncover the unsavory motivations that human beings sometimes have. I want my students to question the motivations behind interpretations and different rhetorics. I want them to understand the positions that politicians take and why they take them.

My thoughts about whether politics should enter the classroom directly are equally contradictory. On the one hand, if political debate cannot take place in the classroom, where should it take place? If one believes, as I do, that the role of criticism is to make the work of literature contemporary by casting it into the light of the present moment, it makes no sense to obstruct its use as a medium of political discussion. Much poststructuralist theory has failed precisely because it has no hold on what is important in our lives today, and any criticism that thwarts the reader's capacity to make literature relevant is not critical. On the other hand, the presence of various political agendas in the classroom has the potential to destroy the teacher-student relationship. Political debate requires freedom of expression beyond the penalties that the authorities can levy, and many phenomena have the potential to become penalties in the classroom. Once a teacher's position is made clear, it has the potential to exact penalties and to apply coercion. Even the most careful teacher may browbeat a student in a debate because it is difficult in politics not to take sides, and once one takes a side coalitions form that place students outside the educational dialogue. Notice that I am not arguing against political debate in the classroom but trying to trace some of its perils. Above all, I am questioning the practice of situating political debate before the monarch. It is not easy to encourage the political nature of the classroom and keep control of its hazards at the same time. My own practice, certainly not one to be recommended as a general technique, is to resist the apolitical politics of theory as well as specific political agendas because the former reduce politics to nothing and the latter coerce those who do not agree with them. I much prefer to encourage a political stance that brings students into a dialogue with works of literature and with each other, marking for them the dispositions of gratitude, apology, and interest that permit conversation to unfold. In the current atmosphere this form of politics hardly seems to meet the qualifications of the political at all because it stresses values of community, dialogue, cooperation, and altruistic interpretive relationships. It works to empower the student, and this among all values is anathema at the present moment; but it is hard to conceive of a successful political body that would not rely on at least a few of these values.

I hope that this politics of interpretation is not deaf and dumb. It gives its ear to the work to listen to what it is saying. It takes what we hear into our experience and talks back, understanding the conversation the best way that we can considering who we are. I know that present-day hatred of the sentimental obstructs us from describing the relationship between interpreters and works as a dialogue. We see such descriptions as nostalgic, anthropomorphic, sentimental, and even humanistic. But how can we think otherwise? How can we talk about something we love otherwise? How can we conceive of teaching otherwise? What kind of classroom leaves no place for the dispositions that make conversation possible?

Cold war theories that describe the impossibility or the stupidity of interpretation turn their backs on the politics of teaching literature. They hold in contempt the kind of work that literature does, and by implication they have disdain for the classroom and students. The argument "against interpretation," so powerfully associated with structuralism and poststructuralism, expresses repulsion for the thought that interpretation might be a medium through which to think as well as for the kinds of reading practiced by most students.[11] For these theorists, reading proves that interpretation is impossible, if rigorously performed, and stupid, if unrigorously performed. It establishes as a model for the political body of the classroom an idea of stupefying virtuosity, in which the teacher returns through increasingly skeptical and unworldly proofs to the idea that his or her students cannot succeed in understanding a work of literature. These teachers most frequently garner this idea of virtuosity to themselves, for career advancement, but even when it is ascribed to literature it ends in frustration. For literature, according to this view, cares nothing for its own virtuosity. Virtuosity is wasted on it, and it makes no apology for it. These theorists hold, in the final analysis, that we can have no

[11] See Christopher Norris's remarks on the poststructuralist disdain for interpretation in his *The Deconstructive Turn: Essays in the Rhetoric of Philosophy* (New York: Methuen, 1984), 163–73.

interest in what literature knows and that we should not spend our time trying to have a conversation with it.

If we listen to the critics against interpretation, we will exchange the kinds of storytelling and talk found in literature for their skeptical theory of language. This theory claims that the possibility of dialogue is an illusion created by a linguistic mirage; and because we cannot find a synthesis between two illusory positions, we should give up trying to fast-talk our way, to interpret our way, across the gulf. We had better, if they are right, call off all interpretation.

But such imperatives remind me of the song by the Gershwins sung by Billie Holiday, which I like to think of as an opposing example of the kind of thinking aloud and conversation that interpretation is:

> You like potatoes,
> and I like potatoes.
> You like tomatoes,
> and I like tomatoes.
> Potatoes, potatoes,
> tomatoes, tomatoes.
> Let's call the whole thing off.
> But, oh, if we call the whole thing off,
> then we must part.
> And, oh, if we ever part,
> then that might break my heart.

The song goes on to fast-talk its way in a homey example of poetic intelligence toward a resolution:

> For we know we
> need each other so we
> better call the calling off off.
> Let's call the whole thing off.

Such resolutions are lost on critics skeptical of interpretation. They believe that we must part because "tomatoes" and "tomatoes" look alike but sound different. But, oh, that might break our hearts.

Better call the calling off off.

6

The Politics of Storytelling Hannah Arendt's *Eichmann in Jerusalem*

Few modern events have stirred the need for recollection and judgment more than the Holocaust. As time passes and witnesses die, however, its memory grows more dim; and legally speaking, the atrocities of Nazi anti-Semitism have remained for the most part unjudged. The Nuremburg trials and the trial of Adolf Eichmann assume great historical significance because they provided concrete occasions for recollecting and judging. The Eichmann trial in particular created a kind of chain reaction of judgment: the judgment of Eichmann gave way to the judgment of anti-Semitism, of Israel, of the Jewish victims, and of the lawyers and the reporters at the trial. The trial also provided an occasion for a multitude of victims to recount their tales of suffering. The judgment of Eichmann welded participants into a chain of responsibility, in which each person was linked to others in the act of recollecting and judging.

This phenomenon is itself rare, if we follow Hannah Arendt's assessment of the modern world. Arendt describes modernity as an epoch little interested in remembrance and afraid of passing judgment. To judge is to subsume a particular experience under a general rule. But people in the modern age hesitate to perform the calculation that requires them to create a general rule to account for a particular event.

Rather, they embrace an amorphous skepticism, remaining suspended between the love of facts and the love of preexisting categories of thinking. They prefer information and formulas to the need to remember and the act of judging; and since information offers little to the experience of memory, and formulas defeat judgment, modern individuals risk losing the ability to learn from experience. Experience is lost between fact and formula. "Unfortunately," Arendt complains, "it seems to be much easier to condition human behavior and make people conduct themselves in the most unexpected and outrageous manner than it is to persuade anybody to learn from experience; that is, to start thinking and judging instead of applying categories and formulas which are deeply ingrained in our mind but whose basis of experience has long been forgotten and whose plausibility resides in their intellectual consistency rather than in their adequacy to actual events" (186–87).[1]

To have experience, we must judge. But to judge, we must first imagine and remember, and in a way that resists the destitution of facts, the easy pattern of formulas, and their skeptical negations. Memory and judgment join in their need to tell an individual story. Stories are richer than simple facts and deeper than the preconceived patterns and cultural myths used to impose order on individual experience, and the value of storytelling for cognition thereby surpasses the contributions of history and philosophy.[2] But to tell a story is not easy in the modern world of cold war rivalries. On the one hand, capitalism speeds up existence. It imposes commercial myths upon us and fractures our stories with its glut of information and advertisements. On the other hand, the rise of totalitarianism works to confound both memory and judgment; according to Arendt, the death camps were made possible only because the totalitarian system stole the power of judgment from both victims and victimizers. Totalitarianism does not want its story to be told; it relies on secrets and condemns its victims to oblivion.

[1] References are to Hannah Arendt, "Personal Responsibility Under Dictatorship," *Listener*, 6 August 1964, 185–87, 205.
[2] See the discussion of Louis O. Mink and of the cognitive value of literature in chapter 1, n.12.

In Hannah Arendt's eyes, the trial of Eichmann in Jerusalem brought about a collision of the many forces defining modernity, and she saw it as an opportunity to confront the modern condition.[3] Her report on the trial is really a political treatise that attempts to describe what can be learned from Eichmann's story. More specifically, she resists modernity by trying to tell the story of Eichmann on trial in a way that passes judgment on the act of judging itself as well as in a way that defeats those forces working to obliterate memory. Her analysis is, in my opinion, one of the most successful characterizations of "the politics of interpretation" in existence, and it is leaps and bounds ahead of anything being written today under the aegis of either deconstruction or the new historicism. It is superior to these schools not only in its mode of analysis, which connects the language of Nazi and Israeli propaganda to specific needs, effects, and historical events, but in her willingness to take an unfashionable position in contemporary debates. Arendt expresses a skeptical attitude about the claims of Nazi brutalizers and Jewish collaborators alike, but her skepticism never overrules her political judgment, which is to say that she does not succumb to the temptation of absolute skepticism. For Arendt knows that if memory and judgment are to be preserved, the craft of politics requires that we take a stand, regardless of the risk to ourselves.

The Nazi movement and Israeli politics collided in the Eichmann trial, and Arendt became caught in the middle. Indeed, while the trial became a situation in which people struggled not to be caught in the middle, Arendt fought for what everyone else feared. She wanted to be precisely in the middle. Her desire to be in the thick of the conflict was partly polemical, but it also derived from her views about memory, storytelling, and judgment. The middle was the vantage point from which she could best tell the story of Eichmann in Jerusalem and render judgment on him. For the act of judging does not seek only to create a general rule to account for particular experience; it imagines the situations of other people. Judging, like any form of understanding, involves first reconciling oneself to the existence of the person or the

---

[3] References are to Hannah Arendt, *Eichmann in Jerusalem* (1963; rev. New York: Viking, 1964).

event that one is judging. It is a matter, Arendt argues, of trying "to be at home in the world."[4]

But who would want to be at home in Eichmann's world, and is it possible to judge a man who has no judgment? Is it possible to sympathize with a person who is incapable of showing sympathy? Finally, how can we understand someone who has no understanding? Memory and judging require human company, but Eichmann cut himself off from the chain of sympathy and responsibility necessary to human beings. Both memory and judging require that a story be told; but Eichmann's story could be told only with the greatest difficulty because telling a story requires that a listener or reader be open to the story. The great test of a story is its ability to attract people who desire to become the next teller of the tale, so that the experience of the story cannot be separated from its passage from person to person. That no one wanted to listen to Eichmann's story in the first place, and that no one wanted to recount it, means that no one wanted either to know or to judge the man. In a sense, people wanted only to forget him.

Recent work on the Holocaust explains just how fragile are both memory and judgment; neither the desire to remember nor the desire to judge protects them in a climate that deliberately perverts them. We know that Hitler saw it as a disgrace to be a jurist, and we have all heard about the impossible choices imposed upon people in the ghettos and in the camps. Arendt argues that the Nazis consistently confounded the act of judgment by forcing their victims to choose the lesser of two evils. If we are confronted by two evils, the argument went, we are required to choose the lesser one, whereas it is irresponsible to refuse the choice. Unfortunately, this logic made decision itself impossible by allowing only those choices most abhorrent to the victim. It also encouraged those who chose the lesser evil to forget that they had in fact chosen evil. Indeed, the Nazis persecuted their victims by confronting them with evil and tempting them to feel responsibility

[4]Hannah Arendt, "Understanding and Politics," *Partisan Review* 20, no. 4 (1953): 377. For an extended analysis of the relation between Arendt's and Kant's theories of judgment, see my *Morals and Stories* (New York: Columbia University Press, 1992), 128–33.

for criminal actions they had no freedom to choose. The totalitarian argument of the lesser evil remains, according to Arendt, "one of the mechanisms built into the machinery of terror and crimes" ("Personal Responsibility," 186).

For a long time our only means of facing this machinery of terror and crime was to repeat in nightmarish fashion the very images that the Nazis had created. The result was a kind of Jewish gothic, a catalogue of images and terrors that represented the camps as the ultimate experience of modern horror. These images were replayed in the media first to inform the public of Nazi crimes and then later for entertainment value; the Holocaust has now evolved into a dramatic source used to boost television ratings and to sell automobiles and soft drinks. The memory of the Holocaust has been eroded by repeating plots and stereotyping both victimizers and victims. Consequently, those who believe that the experience of the Holocaust has value for the future must discover new ways of introducing us to the events. Claude Lanzmann's epic film *Shoah,* for example, deliberately avoids familiar gothic images by asking people to tell their stories and to stand where they once stood. He forges a link in memory and judgment between the past and the present without using the artificial drama now associated with the Holocaust. His film makes the point in images, which others have made in argument, that the Holocaust is not a single event but a word in which the personal experience of a multitude of sufferers resonates.[5]

Neither memory nor judgment is served by a Jewish gothic that requires fate or history to arrange an eternal combat between anti-Semite and Jew. Hannah Arendt learned this lesson in Jerusalem, to her utter surprise. She went there with everyone else expecting to catch the horrible specter of Hitler dancing in Eichmann's eyes. What she found was banality. Arendt portrays Eichmann first and foremost as a

---

[5] *Shoah: An Oral History of the Holocaust. The Complete Text of the Film by Claude Lanzmann* (New York: Pantheon, 1985). See also Sidra DeKoven Ezrahi, *By Words Alone: The Holocaust in Literature* (Chicago: University of Chicago Press, 1980), 2, and Jill Robbins, "The Writing of the Holocaust: Claude Lanzmann's *Shoah*," *Prooftexts* 7 (1987): 249–58.

bureaucrat, and in that image of evil she moves ahead of her time.[6] It was not acceptable in 1961, at least not outside Marxist circles, to portray evil in the character of the functionary, but today we understand and accept the image. The fact that our fictions and moral codes now turn to the character of the businessman to represent vice reveals that we have all come to accept what Arendt called "the banality of evil." In a reversal of some proportions, however, we tend increasingly to stress the radical evil of that figure rather than its baseness, thereby undercutting Arendt's idea of banality and creating a stereotype as dangerous as any other.

But Arendt did not describe Eichmann as a functionary to reveal the radical nature of evil; she found evil in that form only because Eichmann was a functionary who had succumbed to evil. Given her idea of judgment, Arendt's only choice as a reporter at the trial was to try to tell the story of this Eichmann. The choice made her into his involuntary biographer, a situation whose irony did not escape her. Just as an Israeli lawyer could not be expected to defend Eichmann without risking personal harm, a Jew could not be expected to tell his story to the world without inciting the Jewish community to anger. That Arendt chose to tell that story and not relinquish her Jewishness is a tribute to both her courage and her foolishness, for some may doubt whether the story was worth all the personal woe that befell her. The tranquility of her work was invaded by hatred. The company of fellow intellectuals was driven beyond her reach. She lost friends to tell the story of an enemy.

Clearly, Hannah Arendt believed that Eichmann's story should be told, but we may ask why? The answer again turns on Arendt's opinion that the story was a valuable experience from which to learn something about how human beings think. Of the Holocaust, Arendt once said, "in such things there is nothing but *Einzelfälle* [particular

---

[6] And ahead of herself. It apparently needs to be stressed, since many critics continue to cite her *The Origins of Totalitarianism* (1951; rev. New York: Harcourt Brace Jovanovich, 1973), that Arendt shifts her view of evil after her experiences in Jerusalem. The early work is based on the idea of the radicalness of evil, whereas *Eichmann* discovers the worldliness of evil, its banality.

cases]."[7] Eichmann's case fits that description as well, being part of the Holocaust. As Arendt saw it, the Eichmann trial held only one story, and she could not translate it into another one, no matter how ignoble it seemed. To tell another story would in fact be a form of forgetting Eichmann. Arendt saw too well the temptation to be like Eichmann: to become a person who has stopped thinking. It is easy to forget someone who has stopped thinking, but that is the greatest danger. Arendt's book takes the unexpected form of Eichmann's biography precisely because of this threat. Eichmann's story concerns one man being tried in one city, and Arendt had to emphasize its particular nature or risk losing her hold on the politics of the situation.

Indeed, that there were nothing but particular cases in the Holocaust has extraordinary political repercussions. It is precisely the particular that totalitarianism struggles to erase as it applies its generalizing and ideological rhetoric. The immediate response to it often succumbs to the temptation to meet its totalizing movement with another one, thereby becoming only a mirror image of the enemy. Arendt therefore criticizes both the press and the prosecution for presenting the Eichmann case as a model for thinking about fate, history, or anti-Semitism in general: there is "no system on trial," she concludes, "no history or historical trend, no 'ism', anti-semitism for instance, but a person; and if the defendant happens to be a functionary, he stands accused precisely because even a functionary is still a human being, and it is in this capacity that he stands trial. . . . If the defendant were permitted to plead either guilty or not guilty as representative of a system, he would indeed become a 'scapegoat'" ("Personal Responsibility," 186).

Arendt's report, then, focuses on the obstacles to remembrance and judgment created by Eichmann's own stories and by the stories told about him by lawyers, politicians, and other reporters. The latter stories, always prompted by special interests, amount to a form of static that interferes at every turn with the real story of Eichmann's life. Arendt describes the television broadcasts of the trial as being interrupted by "real-estate advertising" and the outbursts, apparently "spontaneous," of the lawyers, complaining about Eichmann's lies. She also criticizes the prosecuting attorney for his showmanship. To the stories of genuine suffering told by the victims, she opposes the prosecutor's staging of the event. In his estimation, the trial should tighten its focus on the crimes of the German people against humanity, on anti-Semitism as a phenomenon, or on racism as such. Again and again he tries to transform the trial into a history lesson on eternal anti-Semitism from Pharaoh to the present. History becomes, in his words, "the bloodstained road traveled by this people," the Jews, and assumes the character of a path necessary to accomplish their destiny (19). In *The Origins of Totalitarianism,* Arendt attacks similar descriptions of Jewish history because they blunt the seriousness of anti-Semitism and conceive of matters human in the most inhuman terms by invoking a supernatural view of history as the cause of actions for which people must be held responsible. Furthermore, in the report on the trial, Arendt complains that such general pictures evade the problem of Eichmann's evil, replacing it with dramas of large and tragic proportions written in the name of such abstractions as destiny and history. These dramas are easy to repeat and to remember, but they have little to do with individual human experience.

Similarly, Ben-Gurion incited Arendt's anger because he announced beforehand those lessons that the trial should teach to "Jews and Gentiles, to Israelis and Arabs, in short, to the whole world" (9). A lesson, or a moral, may come of a story, but if the lesson is told before the story, the story risks not being told. Ben-Gurion's lessons were clear, but Arendt doubted whether they were part of the story. Rather, Ben-Gurion had committed "the sin of trying to make a story come true," to borrow Arendt's remarks on Isak Dinesen, "of interfering with life according to a preconceived pattern, instead of waiting patiently for the story to emerge. . . ."[8] For Ben-Gurion, the trial was supposed to demonstrate that the "Jews had always faced a 'hostile world'" and to implicate the world in the murder of six million Jews: "Let world opinion know this, that not only Nazi Germany was re-

[8] Hannah Arendt, *Men in Dark Times* (New York: Harcourt, Brace and World, 1955), 106.

sponsible for the destruction of six million Jews of Europe" (9–10). In a sense, the trial could come to an end only when it had uncovered the Eichmann in every one of us.

No doubt collective guilt is a powerful political device, but it risks clouding judgment, and it does not serve memory very well because it believes in no particular experience. "Morally speaking," Arendt argues, "it is hardly less wrong to feel guilty without having done something specific than it is to feel free of guilt if one is actually guilty of something" (298). Both actions destroy judgment. Finally, if Eichmann were only one more anti-Semite in the hostile world of eternal anti-Semitism, how could he be judged? His guilt would serve in that case only as a symbol for a collective guilt spread so thin as to have no meaning at all.

In Arendt's opinion, the prosecution's image of Eichmann impeded his exposure to judgment by representing him as a symbol for metaphysical dramas of history and fate. But what distressed her more was the uncanny similarity between this image and Eichmann's own view of himself. For Arendt, Eichmann was, above all else, a man who had stopped thinking. He had adopted the most cliché expressions to describe his life and motivations; he grew elated when he spoke of himself and his destiny, lifted, as it were, by his own petard. Now Arendt discovered that others described not only the defendant but themselves in the same language.

Arendt's commentary on this language is sustained, but her major point may be easily rehearsed and briefly illustrated. It exemplifies what the political analysis of language should consist of, and it deserves to stand as a model for future political interpretation. Arendt exposes again and again the fact that both Eichmann and those speaking on behalf of the Jewish people used a gothic language of destiny and superhuman agency to interpret themselves. Eichmann confessed that "officialese" was his only language, but his confession was only partially true. He was equally well versed in the cliché language of Destiny, History, and Movement. He described himself as a "bearer of secrets," whose hard-luck story it was to be sacrificed to the gods of misfortune (28). He was, moreover, swallowed by history and its grandiose events, for "everything went wrong, my personal affairs as well as my years-long efforts to obtain land and soil for the Jews. I don't know, everything was as if under an evil spell . . ." (50). And as if history and destiny were not sufficient causes for his woes, Eichmann blamed the Nazi movement for his bad luck: "The subject of a good government is lucky, the subject of a bad government is unlucky. I had no luck" (175). "I am not the monster I am made out to be," Eichmann lamented. "I am the victim of a fallacy" (248).

Eichmann represents himself not only as a victim but as an exemplary victim, a special victim unlike any other. He views himself not as ordinary but as radical; he is a person of the kind destined to conduct ultimate meanings. Indeed, Eichmann begins his memoirs by suggesting that his destiny flies above the human world and that his form is a mere envelope containing more powerful forces: "Today . . . I begin to lead my thoughts back to the nineteenth of March of the year 1906, when at five o'clock in the morning I entered life on earth *in the aspect of a human being*" (27; emphasis mine). The trial merely provides Eichmann with the proof of his destiny by setting him apart and marking him with the seal of a unique fate, and he gladly offers himself as a symbol to the world on behalf of the Jews: I propose, he exclaims, "to hang myself in public as a warning example for all anti-Semites on this earth" (24). Here, then, is a man who believes himself victimized by history, fate, and international politics, but who seems all too willing to accept his martyrdom, if only it has the proper symbolic consequences and furthers his own notoriety. So misunderstood by the world in his own eyes, Eichmann simultaneously exculpates himself and offers himself as a symbol of guilt, hoping to achieve through these means an even greater power and agency in world affairs.

The prosecution and press, quite naturally, represented Eichmann as a monster rather than as a buffoon, and they began repeating his eerie and otherworldly images of himself. He was "a perverted, sadistic personality" and "a man obsessed with a dangerous and insatiable urge to kill" (26). Arendt is also guilty to some extent of repeating Eichmann's rhetoric when she describes him as enigmatic and thought-defying, for Eichmann would have liked to have been considered

"thought-defying."[9] More disturbing, the prosecution and government press releases applied Eichmann's victimary rhetoric and his
sense of martyrdom to the Jewish people as well. Eichmann, when
most elated, described himself as a martyr to his idea, and claimed
fascination with the "Jewish question" because he saw in the Jews
fellow idealists. An idealist, according to Eichmann, lived for an idea
and was prepared to sacrifice for that idea everything and everyone.
Eichmann's martyr complex was revealed in his fervent desire to die
for his idea and in his elation before the executioner; but, in fact, the
comparison between Jewish idealism and his own was perverse in
the extreme, and so too was the rhetoric at the trial that represented
the victims of the Holocaust either as fulfilling some grand destiny or
as martyrs to the cause of Israel. The Jews were rarely martyrs, properly speaking, because they did not sacrifice themselves for an idea.
Indeed, they were permitted neither the power nor the dignity of having an idea. Rather, they were sacrificed for the ideas of their mur-
derers. They were killed simply because they were. The Nazis worked
for the most obvious political reasons to eliminate the possibility of
martyrdom, and only a recuperative history designed to restore dignity
and power to the Jewish state could represent the victims as martyrs to
history. Although such revisionary histories lend cohesion to state
politics and are valuable in that respect, they risk masking the fundamentally human and helpless nature of the Jewish victims.

The trial, then, did not sufficiently allow people of flesh and blood to
emerge; rather, it concealed them in a garb of theatrical making, designed to summon political generalities, grandiose movements, and
fateful plots. Nor did the trial allow the stories of the victims to have
their full impact. Perhaps more threatening than the nature of political
theater at the trial was its influence on individual testimony. As the
trial became more of a stage, Arendt concludes, the events grew more
tragic in the dramatic sense, but they were inevitably less personal,

[9] Without suggesting that skepticism creates the political disasters of this era, I note the
remarkable similarity between Eichmann's psychology and the soft psychology of skeptics who relish their difference from others and the defiant nature of their thought. The
inability to locate skeptical claims in the world creates for the skeptic an ultimate destiny
worlds apart from the impoverished and mundane conditions of the simple believer.

individual, and human. "As witness followed witness and horror piled upon horror," Arendt explains, the people "sat there and listened in public to stories they would hardly have been able to endure in private, when they would have had to face the storyteller" (8). The fourth wall of the stage imposed itself between witness and audience, making the stories more bearable but blunting their ability to communicate as well as their essentially human character.

Arendt understands stories and knows that they exist only in communications from person to person, because an essential ingredient of any story is the bond created between speaker and listener or writer and reader. This dialogue makes the story a fertile ground for judgment, for speaker and listener exchange sympathies and positions through the medium of language. Thus, Arendt's account of Zindel Grynszpan's testimony at the trial focuses on the inherent power of his story and the directness of its telling (227–30). Grynszpan recounts a day in his life in the autumn of 1938, when he and his family were deprived of German nationality and expelled to Poland. Some twelve thousand Jews were processed that day by the Germans and driven to the train station through the streets, black with people shouting, *"Juden raus* to Palestine."* From the station, they were transported to the Polish border, and there the SS drove them like beasts for over a mile until they crossed the border and were interned by the Polish authorities in a village of six thousand—twelve thousand added to six thousand, and the majority had not eaten in four days. Arendt emphasizes that Grynszpan's story did not even remotely resemble a "dramatic moment," but it nevertheless conveyed, through its shining honesty, the needless destruction of his twenty-seven years of life in less than twenty-four hours.

A story's objective is to convey human experience, but its silences and the speaker's inability to continue are equally parts of the storytelling experience, and in the case of the catastrophic events of the Holocaust the storyteller's own emotional fragmentation may be the most powerful indication of the events. One of the most moving and memorable scenes of Claude Lanzmann's film concerns Abraham Bomba's story about cutting women's hair in the gas chambers.[10] He tries to tell

[10] Lanzmann, *Shoah: The Complete Text*, 111–17.

the story of a friend, a good barber, who saw his wife and his sister come into the death chamber. The women did not know that they were there to die, and the barber could not tell them. He tried to cut their hair more slowly, a minute longer, a second longer, just to hug and kiss them, because he knew that he would never see them again. Abraham Bomba breaks down, when he tries to tell the story. He turns from the camera and covers his face with his hands. The story stops and starts, interrupted this time not by noise, commercials, or political announcements but by the force of the story itself, by its own rhythms and the emotions dictating its form in a face-to-face encounter between human beings.[11]

It is crucial to stress that Abraham Bomba's story does not fail precisely because it stops and starts. For in Bomba's emotional interruptions resides the story's humanity. It is equally crucial to recognize that the trial did not fail in Arendt's eyes, despite all the obstacles to memory and judgment, for these obstacles were put in place by human hands. The stories of Abraham Bomba and Adolf Eichmann stand at perverse extremes; but both are integral to the experience of the Holocaust, if it is to be remembered and judged, if its stories are to be told. Both stories require a form of patience, although of a very different kind: we must be willing to pass the story from teller to teller, to have the patience both to listen to the story and to retell it, and to accept the responsibilities of becoming a storyteller. Storytelling engages the patient art of thinking, for thinking is an act of imagining from the standpoint of someone else, an act, therefore, fundamentally of conversation and communication. It implies the idea of a tradition and the desire to be at home and among others in the human community, but it is too rare in our day. The Nazi movement did all that it could to crush our patience with these stories, and now our modern urge to rush through life demands that we shorten our stories or transform them into blockbusters. Meanwhile, the skeptical temperament acts to preserve the void created by these movements, questioning general politi-

---

[11] Falling into silence, like the act of fast-talking discussed in chapter 5, is another characteristic of dialogue. Both confront the possibility that conversation might end but resist it, the first by incorporating the gulf in the conversation into the dialogue and the second by throwing speech across it.

cal narratives and denouncing the viability of particular facts. Indeed, skepticism has become the modern blockbuster. Its logic resides in totalitarian and capitalist aspirations alike, pitting huge dramas of paranoia and suspicion against our desires to hear the real story about the evil and goodness of human beings.

These forces, called modern by Arendt, would seem to condemn the story of the Holocaust to oblivion.[12] But fortunately oblivion is not so easily attainable. "Nothing human is that perfect," Arendt writes, "and there are simply too many people in the world to make oblivion possible" (232–33).

That we commit to telling these stories is, humanly speaking, all that memory and judgment require of us.

[12] Although this is not the place, a criticism of Arendt's view of modernity could be developed by tracing it from Georg Lukács through a certain Walter Benjamin, and asking to what extent it partakes of a form of romantic nostalgia for the past. This past is always represented as somehow more human than the present, but we may question whether this description is not a denial of human properties, since the modern character remains, arguably, as human as any found in the past. A second and more productive variety of nostalgia found in Arendt has, in my view, little to do with this first one. It concerns the politics by which skeptical thought works to find itself "at home in the world." See the analysis of fast-talking in chapter 5, and chapter 7, n.15 for further discussion of nostalgia.

7

Conclusion
Toward a Post–Cold War Criticism

When Gorbachev began his first efforts at de-Stalinization, more than one political commentator remarked that the Soviet Union had finally entered the postwar era. This appraisal may have come as a surprise to many of us. We are accustomed to viewing World War II as a distant event, having little or no influence on present schools of thought.

For the literary critics of our generation, however, this appraisal must have meant that a rapid acceleration in history had occurred. Not only has modern criticism not faced the influence of the postwar era, it has rather avidly sought to avoid it by sinking its intellectual roots in the nineteenth century, especially in late romanticism. The link between our postsomething schools of thought—the poststructuralists and postmoderns—and the postwar era has been concealed by creating a more visible link between the postromantic and the postmodern, as any good student of postmodernism will immediately understand. I have been suggesting, however, that epithets such as "poststructuralist" and "postmodern" work as guarded allusions to the postwar world, and that much of the coherence that these intellectual movements possess arises specifically from their avoidance of present day political realities born of the postwar climate. My argument has been that criticism today is a cold war criticism and that it is bordering on failure. Criticism has no future when it has no present. It has no present when it turns its back on its contemporary political and ethical context.

The New Criticism, structuralism, poststructuralism, and deconstruction are our most visible postwar criticisms. If asked to define literary theory, most professors of literature would mention ideas and thinkers associated with these schools of thought. But these movements are products of a particular situation having to do with the status of the university in the postwar world. They are, first and foremost, academic criticisms. It has become commonplace to associate the New Critical technique of close reading and French explication de texte with the historical need to find a means to teach literature to the burgeoning population of college students that emerged during the postwar years. Confronted by so many students in the classroom, teachers snipped the titles from poems and ignored their histories to create a method of reading that needed, as it were, no prerequisites. But this method also blinded students to the contexts in which works of literature are made and read.

The usual interpretation is that the invention of the method of close reading caused a change in the study of literature. But we have not faced the fact that this method may not have been the root cause of this change but merely an effect of a larger political trend in the university. This trend is too large to study here, so I will remain largely within the usual interpretation, but what I have in mind is a description of the increasing isolation of the university from contemporary political and social contexts, a locking, as it were, of the university in the deep freeze of the cold war era. The pursuits of intellectual life, as described in university classrooms, have little to do with the daily life of students and the politics of our communities; and, unfortunately, when the university does make a direct political contribution to the non-academic world, its involvement is usually retrograde. Consider some exceptions to the isolation of the university in recent years. The protest against the Vietnam War is one obvious case. But this protest was a student movement and not a university one. Another case is the increasing involvement of the university in weapons research and the gathering of military intelligence. Here, at least, the university has awakened from its dogmatic slumber to participate in world events, although, ironically, it finds itself working in cooperation with the military. A final case involves big business. The university research most oriented toward present-day reality is concerned with helping business to create a market. It therefore cooperates in maintaining the beliefs necessary to that market instead of studying how these beliefs create and increase our interest.

In the humanities especially the flight into a monumentalizing historicism exaggerates this general isolation. I wish to stress that I am referring to new brands of historical study and not to the idea of historiography in itself, which connects academic disciplines to everyday life rather than monumentalizing itself. The humanities today operate more and more under the banner of a new kind of history, and their devotion to it has allowed them to submerge themselves in the past. Each discipline now possesses a history of itself, and this historicism has begun to exercise an increasing power over the ways in which the disciplines define their intellectual pursuits. Its ruling myth is that historicism will lead to an explanation of the present, but there is always more history to be written or rewritten, and we never quite make it to the modern applications, the effect being that historical study fragments history and excuses the insulation of the humanities from current political and ethical realities. The new historicism, for example, even though it is blatantly concerned with ideology and politics, encourages insulation of political thought because it lodges a cold war view of ideology in the past, usually in minor episodes and catchy anecdotes of the English Renaissance, thereby playing out whatever critique it might possess at a safe distance from the present political scene. Its relation to current events is at best symbolic.[1]

Much critical theory today is part of this trend. It is academic in the extreme, and it has consequently rendered itself academic. But the university was the first to render itself academic. Let me explore briefly some of the manifestations of the failure of criticism today. It is a failure found on many fronts.

---

[1] Despite the hostility expressed in the new historicism toward Ronald Reagan, especially in the writings of Stephen Greenblatt, it is worth considering that the anecdotal style of this school emerged at the same time that Reagan was developing a political use of anecdote in which general claims are driven by eccentric and memorable examples.

A first case might examine the ascendancy of the new three unities. We are in an age as dogmatic as the Neoclassical period, where conventions such as the three unities strangled originality and new thought. No attempt could be made to represent the contemporary situation because the conventions of representation were too rigid. Our three unities are the triumvirate Freud, Marx, and Nietzsche, and cold war critics have used them to establish a set of rigid laws governing the nature of language. For more than twenty years these oligarchs have ruled the state of literary criticism in the United States, and their hand has been severe. Many claims are made for their radicalism, and they may have been radical at one time, but there is nothing radical about them today. First they were called the ultimate "modern" thinkers. Now they are the ultimate "postmodern" thinkers. Their stock keeps rising, but only because the investors are too conservative and too fat to invest in anything new. Freud-Marx-Nietzsche is a blue-chip investment. It is like a major corporation that manufactures soap powder or soft drinks. The purpose of the company is to make profits, and to do it we must all use more soap and consume more and more soft drinks. Poor Marx may be the only exception here. He is a bit too nostalgic to make the transition from modern to postmodern. He believed in politics, so we sometimes replace him with the formalist Sausurre in order to make certain that there is no danger of connecting criticism with political ideas.

During and immediately after World War II the fates of Freud, Marx, and Nietzsche were different. They were highly charged politically. Marxism was at the heart of current events. The split among Marxists between the pro-Stalinists and the anti-Stalinists, the controversies raging in the *Partisan Review* and elsewhere, the cold war, McCarthyism, and the birth of the conservative movement in American politics assured Marx a prominent position in everyday debate. Marxism then stood to the left, but today Marxism is essentially a liberal parlor game, played for amusement in university classrooms and academic journals. It has been stripped of everything that made it

---

On the relation between the new historicism and Reaganomics, see the discussion in chapter 2.

politically controversial in order to render it safe for consumption in college classrooms. It is advertised as new-and-improved, with a different flavor, but it has become one more product on the supermarket shelf of academic criticism. Indeed, Marxism has little vitality in the United States outside of the university. It is now largely a product for academic consumption.

During the same period Nietzsche was connected to the Nazi's recipe for world domination. After varying the recipe for thirty years, a new-and-improved version of Nietzsche came out: Nietzsche, the radical, the hero of the counterculture. I understand from reading *Semiotext(e)* that sometime in the 1970s Nietzsche was seen wearing long hair and sporting a Fu Manchu mustache.[2] Now we even have Nietzsche the feminist, an idea that makes the mind boggle. But today "Nietzsche" is largely shorthand for a type of linguistic analysis that labels aesthetics and ethics as ideologies concealing their stakes in power. Although supposedly of great use to political analysis, this version of Nietzsche is itself depoliticized because it conceals the stakes that Nietzsche's philosophy had in the intellectual rivalries of his time and in the history of world power. It has, moreover, rendered formulaic one of our most iconoclastic thinkers.

Freud has suffered a similar fate. At first, Freud was anathema to the Marxists and the Nietzscheans. He was a thinker whom the Nazis and fascists had tried to discredit. The political divisions between Freudians and Marxists were also deep; and those who embraced Freud did so with an understanding of what his Jewishness meant in the context of the period. Freud's own methods were perfected between the two world wars, when his experience with victims of battle fatigue forced him to make his famous leap beyond the pleasure principle. His clinical methods were used again to heal soldiers after World War II. In short, the theories of Freud are inextricably bound to the history of the world wars.[3] But now that his ideas have been surpassed clinically by Ameri-

[2] I refer to the back cover of *Semiotext(e)* 2, no. 3 (1977), which pictures "Nietzsche's Return" and the welcoming refrain, "Beyond Freud and Marx, brother Nietzsche at the dawn of the counter-culture."

[3] This topic has been largely ignored in Freudian studies, even though the return to Freud asserts the association. Jacques Lacan's work is peppered with references to concentra-

can experimental and cognitive science, his work on human behavior, anxiety, and emotions has become less important than his metapsychology, and he remains, a shadow of his former self, as one more recipe in the critical cookbook. Literary critics want to know nothing about current scientific thought, and they content themselves with Freud's ideas because he has a literary flair, exhibits a fondness for mythological expressions, and can be used to support the modern obsession with language. Psychoanalysis also makes it possible to avoid direct, political analysis because it interiorizes anything resembling the political in terms of intrapersonal conflicts and ego projections.[4] The value that Freud did possess originally has been lost by mixing him with everyone else in the postmodern potage of criticism.

The three unities holding criticism together today are not modern, and in no way postmodern. Marx died in 1883, Nietzsche in 1900, Freud in 1939. Literary critics behave as if nothing new has happened in economics, philosophy, and psychology since these dates.

Recently, the controversies surrounding Martin Heidegger and Paul de Man have forced literary critics to think about their relation to the postwar era.[5] Criticism may be experiencing a period of de-Stalin-

tion camps and to "the cold war of interpretative demonstrations" (*Ecrits,* 16). See also his remarks on the "concentrational" language of existentialism in "The Mirror Stage" and "Aggressivity in Psychoanalysis," in his *Ecrits: A Selection,* trans. Alan Sheridan (New York: Norton, 1977), 1–7, 8–29, esp. 6 and 16, and on the gulags of the Soviet Union in the "Preface" to Anika Lemaire, *Jacques Lacan,* trans. David Macey (London: Routledge and Kegan Paul, 1977), vii–xv, esp. ix.

[4] See, for example, the idea of "politics" produced by Jean-François Lyotard's blend of Freudian and Heideggerian thought, in his *Heidegger and "the jews,"* trans. Andreas Michel and Mark Roberts (Minneapolis: University of Minnesota Press, 1990), which describes "the jews" as a general category of the "forgotten," produced by primary repression, that awakens the ego's desire for violence in the form of a secondary repression against Jews, blacks, and other minorities. The world stage becomes the psyche, and there is nothing to do about violence and oppression, except to put the world on the couch. Thus politics merges with pop psychology.

[5] It is remarkable that both the Heidegger and de Man affairs of 1987 and 1988 surfaced at the very moment in history when the world was thinking most intensely about the postwar order. In neither case were the discoveries of Nazi connections entirely new, for Heidegger's relation to the Nazis was open knowledge, and rumors had been circulating for years in the case of de Man. Perhaps their collaboration became important only as a

ization as well. But to date our exercises in self-reflection have been mediocre. Indeed, if whole wings of critical thought rely on the positions of Martin Heidegger and Paul de Man, as they appear to, the future of political criticism is dubious. De Man's theories are, of course, of the most obscurantist and arcane variety. They cannot be applied to political reality, and those who claim the contrary must make a long stretch to prove it. They cite his ideas on aesthetic ideology and on language power, but his analysis is wholly metaphorical. His theories have sufficient power to tickle the brains of a happy few, but they do not have the purchase to say anything about our world as it is. When de Man's collaborationist writings were discovered, his obscurantism revealed its motivation. His theories are so difficult to apply to politics because he had much to conceal politically, and it is unfortunate that his ideas have been one of the major means by which critical theorists hide out politically. De Man fled to the university after the war and hid his politics. Likewise, literary criticism as a genre fled to the university to escape politics.

The Heidegger affair leads one to similar conclusions, but they are more frightening. Heidegger's thought, of course, condemns the political and ethical use of literature as the greatest ideological danger; and predictably the reaction to the Heidegger affair by almost every major poststructuralist critic has been intentionally depoliticized.[6] Philippe Lacoue-Labarthe, for example, has defended Heidegger as the great thinker of the destruction of Western humanism and its myth of progress. In the apocalypse at Auschwitz, according to Lacoue-Labarthe's outlandish claims, nothing more or less than the essence of the West is

---

sign of the thawing of the cold war. For during the height of the cold war, it was less important to be a Nazi sympathizer than a communist. With the melting away of the old order, the political irresponsibility of Heidegger and de Man became visible and compelling.

[6] Heidegger's fear of combining aesthetics and politics belongs to what I called in chapter 2 the era of propaganda, the period in the cold war during which the battle was shifted to the domain of linguistic and technological competition. Heidegger's thought abounds with fears about technology, of course, but we usually do not consider how they relate to his period, preferring to see them in a romantic light. Similarly, his attitude toward forms of pure and impure speech fits in with the general apprehension about propaganda felt during the period.

revealed.[7] Heidegger, more than any other philosopher, Lacoue-Labarthe argues, allows us to understand the terror that is the West. Auschwitz is no longer the product of the Nazis, whom Heidegger supported, but the product of Western civilization. Apparently, we have no business throwing stones at the Nazis and the great Heidegger. They were only fulfilling the destiny of the West. They were victims of Western civilization, and Heidegger, for one, knew it, although he was powerless to do anything about it. Are we to blame the poor tragic Heidegger if he overcompensated for his helplessness just a little by trying to set himself up as the dictator of the University of Freiburg?

Jean-François Lyotard in *Heidegger and "the jews"* concocts a similar argument about the psychology of the West, although he makes much of his differences with Lacoue-Labarthe. In the specific case of Heidegger, Lyotard's first move is to discount as indices of the "political" those gestures, symbols, and actions by which people usually identify themselves with political groups. Thus, Heidegger's thought is more important for an understanding of his politics than the fact that he paid dues to the Nazi party and denounced its "enemies." But what Lyotard really means when he talks about Heidegger's thought is his writing, which allows Lyotard to swing the argument in the direction of poststructuralist linguistics. This writing exists outside of nazism because Heidegger is thrown "much further than Nazism, well beyond and outside it" by the unbearable anxiety that seizes human destiny, and his thought can therefore bear no resemblance to that espoused by the SS men with their "impeccable boots and dangling cigarettes" (64). "Heidegger," Lyotard writes, "was not a Nazi like Rosenberg, Krieck, or Goebbels" (64). But would Lyotard, connoisseur of difference,

---

[7] Philippe Lacoue-Labarthe, *Heidegger, Art, and Politics,* trans. Chris Turner (Cambridge, Mass.: Basil Blackwell, 1990), 29, 35, 37. Lacoue-Labarthe agrees with Heidegger's assessment that the *technē* condemned by Platonic philosophy asserts itself in modern technology, the consequence being that the technology of the Final Solution is the natural flowering of Western art.

The book that started the Heidegger affair and against which Lacoue-Labarthe and others are reacting is, of course, Victor Farias's *Heidegger and Nazism,* trans. Paul Barrell et al. (Philadelphia: Temple University Press, 1989). For an additional sample of responses, see the essays by Gadamer, Habermas, Derrida, Levinas, and Blanchot in *Critical Inquiry* 15, no. 2 (1989).

claim that Krieck was a Nazi like Goebbels, or that Eichmann was a Nazi like Rosenberg, or that any one Nazi was a Nazi like all the others? The point is not really that Heidegger should be defended because he was not a cliché Nazi. Lyotard's point seems to be that Heidegger cannot be a cliché Nazi (as if anyone ever was) because he was a great writer. We have merely confused with "nazism," Lyotard claims, this profound writer's struggle with *Verfallenheit,* with "the anamnesis to which thought is destined" (63–64). In sum, Lyotard evades Heidegger's political situation by describing him in terms of the most romantic clichés about poets and writers—clichés, moreover, that Heidegger used to describe and to defend himself.[8]

In the last few years, despite the fact that they have had their hands full defending both Heidegger and de Man, poststructuralist theorists have turned to the topic of nationalism. What have they learned? They have discovered that the universal claims of philosophy, and of German philosophy in particular, conceal a celebration of nationalism. In short, philosophical thought is always reducible to the national interests of the writer and the quest for power. Tell me, would Heidegger in his most fanatical moment have disagreed with this analysis? Would the Nazi propaganda machine bent, for example, on demonstrating that Jewish thought is dangerous and nonassimilable, that it is never, in short, anything other than *Jewish* thought, and that it is never concerned with anything other than an apparent grasping for power and money, have wished to contradict the theorists here? So the critique of philosophy has come to a matter of nationalism. Everything philosophical is corrupt. Intellectual life, ethics, and art are only a mad scramble for power.

Modern criticism celebrates differences at every turn, but when it comes to national differences the desire for difference vanishes. We

---

[8] If it is not obvious, my ultimate point about the reaction to the Heidegger and de Man affairs is that no one has had the courage to write about them in the way that Arendt wrote about Eichmann. The men themselves and their particular histories are effaced, and critics pour over their ironic prose for answers. The effect is similar to what would have happened if Arendt had refused to cover the trial or to trace Eichmann's various historical encounters with Jewish and Nazi leaders and had argued that we must do nothing but perform close readings of his memoirs in order to reveal his ambivalences about anti-Semitism.

cannot base politics on geographical enclaves and remain politically correct. We must universalize politics to free it from such differences. Only by stripping politics of desire and interest, only by purifying it philosophically, modern critics argue, may we avoid the dreaded will to power that infects our lamentable species.

The reduction of all claims for thought to the will to power is championed today by many, and it is seen as a liberating political gesture. Indeed, it defines the political gesture par excellence in critical circles. But this gesture has a notorious and right-wing history. It drives one to political conservatism and cuts off the intellect. It locks one in the deep freeze of cold war paranoia. More significantly, its abstract and pseudo-political rhetoric excuses one from political action. How can we repeat this ideology without falling into its grasp?

The fact that critics so easily excuse Heidegger and de Man today is astounding. We make grand claims for the autonomy of thought or the independence of the history of ideas to conceal their irresponsibility. We continue using their formulas and phrases to churn out yet another reading, and this fact exposes the truth that we have no real political context at present. These men can be saved only by relinquishing the little that remains of our political conscience.

The intellectual scene immediately following World War II was different. Literary critics were aware of and wrote about world events, and literature guided them in thinking about these events.[9] Literary journals were relevant to the present, and intellectuals had not yet begun to closet themselves in the university. But the new economic situation following the war led to more academic positions, and many intellectuals were lost to the university, where they began to pine away

[9] The current scene has few such intellectuals, Edward Said and Noam Chomsky numbering among those who have made the transition from the academy to a larger context. I am, incidentally, in substantial agreement with Said's description of the present, non-political community of literary critics as elaborated in "Opponents, Audiences, Constituencies," in *The Anti-Aesthetic: Essays on Postmodern Culture,* ed. Hal Foster (Port Townsend, Wash.: Bay Press, 1983), 135–59. Said argues that critical theory and literary study remain marginal to our society because they define the political in opposition to actual politics, and he stresses, moreover, that this definition of the political collaborates with the conservative tendencies of the "Age of Reagan." His solution is to intervene through literary interpretation in the modern political scene.

and to inbreed. A cold war climate of terror, fear, and paralysis drove others to turn away from political thought. The result is the narrow academic criticism of our day. Those who remained outside the university—with some notable exceptions—had neither the intellectual gifts nor the artistic ability to continue the critical effort. Today our intelligent publications outside of academia continue to be political, but they have been compromised intellectually. The Heidegger and de Man affairs pitted journalistic and academic critics against each other, and the results revealed some disturbing facts about the present intellectual scene. The academic critics complained bitterly that the journalists could not begin to understand the ideas of these men, and that the arguments of the journalists were error-ridden, incompetent, and unjust. This was certainly the case, attesting to the lamentable condition of thought in nonacademic circles. The journalists countered by arguing that the academic critics were blinded by obscure discourse, had given up their principles to buy a place in the ivory tower, and had no sense of the horrors brought about by the ideas held by Heidegger and de Man. This was also certainly the case, attesting to the inability of academic critics to comprehend anything remotely resembling a political argument or an act of conscience. Literary theory today is divided by this sorry schism. If it is political, it is not rigorous; if it is rigorous, it is not political. Theory is out of touch with political debate.[10]

It is not surprising, then, that almost all of our major critics have announced that theory is dead. They ought to know because they killed it. The irony is that theory has been dead for a long time, and they are only now showing the body in a last-ditch effort to keep center stage. The body is as smelly as an old cheese, and the flesh is mummified. Its teeth were never intact, although everyone pretended that they were sharp. They have now propped up the body for special exhibit. They point at it and say, "Yes, you see, theory is dead." It smiles back at them with the clownish grin of an old-fashioned laboratory skeleton.

Alas, theory is dead. Long live theory. We are told that it died

[10] Politics becomes that place where critical theory reaches its limits. See the discussion of Harriet Beecher Stowe in chapter 5.

because it was not practical. You cannot practice this kind of theory, the critics now theorize. Besides, everything is practice in the first place, they say, so there is every reason in the world to dispense with this allegory of practice called theory and return to the heart of things. The problem is that what they call the heart of things is the same old pile of bones. They call it politics, but it has little to do with the political. Lately, they have taken to calling it ethics, but it has little to do with ethics. The ethics underlying cold war critical theory is most visible in its preoccupation with the violence of language.[11] Literary criticism, in its attempts to express the ways in which language violates its objects, makes contact with the ethical tradition because it defends, in spite of itself, the moralistic desire for social harmony. The metaphors used by criticism today propose a view of society as a coherent political body in which moral practices can be achieved, and this view means that criticism belongs to the history of ethics. But, in the final analysis, such descriptions are too charitable toward the ethical metaphors of the present literary theory. The important thing to say is that the move to the metaphorical level, to the symbolism of language, already represents a failure to deal with the ethics of our present reality, no matter how good our intentions.

Let me conclude by treading where angels dare not and speak for a moment about the future of criticism, about what I fear will be a continuation of this ethical and political symbolism—about the failure of criticism, therefore—and about some directions in which criticism might go if we desire to bring it more successfully into the sphere of our daily lives.

Not too long ago a major critic, who shall go nameless, was heard to say that only three issues remain in literary theory: race, gender, and class. It is remarkable that these important issues always come in threes. Will they become our new, new three unities? Race, gender, and class represent the possibility of bringing criticism into contact with everyday life, and we should defend and celebrate the trend; but its effect will be retrograde if we use these categories, as I fear that we will, to maintain a political metaphor in criticism that need not be acted

[11] See my *Ethics of Criticism* (Ithaca, N.Y.: Cornell University Press, 1988).

upon. Already, in fact, the forces of the market and of academic politics have begun to have an influence. Critics are grinding out essays on race, gender, and class. The academic publishing world is in a fever. These books and essays all have political agendas, but rarely does the writer have the nerve to spell out the issues and make proposals. Instead, we find an idle and illusory political rhetoric that encourages abstraction and self-congratulation rather than action. I anticipate more and more of the same under the banner of our new three unities.

On race, I fear that we will see book after book that exposes racist tendencies and elaborates little allegories, very safe ones, announcing that racism is evil. But these narratives will be for the most part politically feeble and out of touch with the important realities at the cause of racism today. Race, gender, and class are not themes like any other. They are political, and race especially is an issue where academics should be able to do something. We are the nation's educators, and the minority issue defines a domain where education is crucial. Yet not enough is being done. Not one of our postmodern theorists has written a viable pedagogical theory, let alone one against racism. Not one has published anything of weight about the nuts and bolts of trying to educate our minority populations. Our grand thinkers leave such "details" to the instructors, half-time faculty, and graduate students who do the work of teaching in the classroom everyday. That our major critical theorists have ignored the practical issues surrounding race, while harping on the rhetoric of race, reveals that they have no sense of politics and no genuine commitment.

Gender. If we speak about the future of criticism and its ethics, we must name feminism as the movement of greatest significance. But I, for one, have certain trepidations about the coming years. Feminism has been for the last two decades the most political and ethical criticism. Now it seems to be losing direction. I see more and more "readings," created to fill in the history of sexism in good academic fashion.[12] The feminist essay risks becoming a genre with its own set of

---

[12] As I make clear in chapter 5, I do not underestimate the symbolic value of interpretation for creating an ethical and aesthetic atmosphere that may influence interpreters and readers to the good. My argument here is more concerned with the lack of activism on the current theoretical scene and the anomaly of that absence *given* the political rhetoric.

mandatory references and obligatory rhetorical phrasings. The academic publishing industry is wild about feminist books. Its enthusiasm for the product promises, I fear, to do for feminism what the postwar employment boom in the university did for literary criticism. If feminist theory is to remain a force in the future, it must resist the temptations of academic rhetoric and university politics and develop more ways to reach men and women outside of the university. Most important, it needs to theorize the interaction between private and public spheres.[13] Feminist criticism has become largely a device serving the self-fashioning impulses of individuals in academia rather than a political program. It must discover a way of incorporating its concerns into the public sphere, unless its politics is to rely solely on the metaphor of "trickling down" so popular in the 1980s.

Class. What can result here, given the present academic environment, other than a rehashing of Marxism? All hope for a vital criticism of social and economic hierarchies depends on our ability to restructure Marxism or to move beyond it toward a political version of cultural studies.[14] In all probability, we will have to abandon Marxism as a label and a methodology, and it will be necessary to exchange terms such as "class" and "ideology" for a vocabulary more appropriate to the social and economic forms of the twentieth and twenty-first centuries. Most important, whatever cultural studies becomes, if it becomes anything, it must resist the hatreds and prejudices of traditional radical politics. A political criticism that mocks politics, disdains community, holds the middle class in contempt, underestimates the

[13] On the necessity of separating private and public spheres, see Chantal Mouffe, "Feminism, Citizenship, and Radical Democratic Politics," in *Feminists Theorize the Political,* ed. Judith Butler and Joan W. Scott (New York: Routledge, 1992), 369–84, and Maurizio Passerin d'Entrèves, "Hannah Arendt and the Idea of Citizenship," in *Dimensions of Radical Democracy,* ed. Chantal Mouffe (London: Verso, 1992), 145–68. This latter collection contains many important reflections on the need to change current philosophical thinking about democracy, community, and citizenship.

[14] For a cogent analysis of the future of Marxism and radical politics, see John McGowan, "Can Marxism Survive?," *Southern Humanities Review* 23, no. 3 (1989): 241–52, and his *Postmodernism and Its Critics* (Ithaca, N.Y.: Cornell University Press, 1991). I also recommend Gayatri Chakravorty Spivak's remarks about post-Marxism in the interviews collected in *The Post-Colonial Critic,* ed. Sarah Harasym (New York: Routledge, 1990).

importance of civil liberties and individual rights, and looks down on popular forms of expression cannot expect to have much influence on the United States of today or tomorrow.

In addition to the recommendation that we redirect the study of race, gender, and class toward our daily lives, I have four other suggestions to make in order to guide criticism into the post–cold war age.

1. We are bound in this age of suspicion to be skeptical. Skepticism is an integral part of modern consciousness, and we cannot do without a healthy skepticism, especially since we find ourselves living in a world in which political mistrust seems necessary to maintain the smallest margin of political activity. But skepticism cannot provide a firm basis for either political or ethical action. We must place our natural skepticism in the service of something and not allow it to be directed to ends willy-nilly by the force of our own exhaustion. The history of recent philosophical and literary skepticism is the story of an exhaustion that turns inward toward its own representation, making supreme virtues of its own loss, guilt, self-doubt, and lack of energy. Skepticism has become a mode of self-fashioning rather than a means to knowledge about the world and human society.

2. Literary criticism needs to take account of what politics really is, which means, first of all, that we need to understand that politics takes place in the world, and that in taking this place, it risks itself. Politics confronts the consequences of the positions that it takes; there are no politics if there are no consequences. Rather than avoiding consequences by reinventing politics as a trope of negative freedom or of the high moral ground, criticism in the future should work to support a positive politics that selects its interests, purposes, actions, and languages according to needs, beliefs, and ideals. At the general level, this means that criticism needs to embrace politics as that craft by which human beings attempt to make a home in the world. At the particular level, this means that criticism needs to define politics in terms of everyday usage and life; international, national, and community issues; citizenship; inclusive justice; the trends of seasonal elections; and party platforms.

3. Criticism needs to include within its province once more life-affirming principles in addition to the ascetic and skeptical ones that it

has come to embrace. Pleasure, beauty, knowledge, and the world (both as nature and human experience) should have a place in the language of criticism. I mention beauty above all as a value that has been systematically banished from critical discourse since the end of World War II. Our current preoccupation with the sublime, for example, redefines art, literature, and morality in terms of terror, cruelty, unintelligible questions, and death drives—cold war emotions if there ever were any. Kant argued that beauty, not the sublime, is the symbol of morality, and he might have added that it has its place in politics as well. Aesthetics possesses ideological dimensions, like everything else, but in it consists as well our awareness of our own bodies, emotions, feelings, and beauty, and these values, so important to the vast majority of people, need to be included along with ascetic and skeptical values in our critical languages. Literary critics who abandon their fondness for storytelling, beauty, aesthetic pleasure, language, and human talk about them willfully estrange themselves from a large part of the world in which they live.

4. Literary criticism should uphold a reverence for our inner lives. We have learned that the self is not a self-contained, autonomous power. Now we need to understand that the interdependence of human beings that constitutes our subjectivity does not preclude the possibility of agency, private feelings, and an inner life. It is from this inner life and our desire to protect it and those friends and relatives close to it that our strongest political and ethical impulses spring. The many components of this inner life must be allowed their place in critical and literary language: spirituality, religion, conscience, nostalgia, family, community, the world of belongings, friendship, motherhood, fatherhood, companionship, respect, love, and eroticism are among the many values that hold people together as well as tear them apart. Recent criticism has labeled such values as too provincial or too ideologically interested and so condemned them to oblivion; but art and literature have not heard about their death, and they continue to make of them major subjects and concerns.

A criticism that has lost touch with its contemporary politics and context is a failed criticism. Our criticism has failed because it has no hold on what is important in our lives today. We do not need a postsomething criticism. We need a modern criticism for the modern day. A modern criticism is not one that tries to dress up works of literature in the garments of old philosophies. There is nothing charming in such masquerades. They have a certain nostalgic appeal, it is true, like a nineteenth-century painting that puts Napoleon in Caesar's robes, but modern criticism has no business serving nostalgia.[15] Nostalgia is anti-modern. It is insufferable in literature, and although critics have always had a greater fondness for the past than writers, nostalgia is just as destructive in criticism as it is in literature, perhaps more so because criticism rarely possesses the depth of literature.

A modern criticism is one that makes the work of literature contemporary by casting it into the light of the present moment. We read only those works of literature that we can read at our moment in history. Fortunately, we are always able to read a large number, owing to our ability to identify with works of literature and to make them relevant to our lives and times. A criticism that thwarts our capacity to make literature relevant by dressing it up in old clothes is not criticism. It is antiliterature. It is antipolitical and antiethical as well. It has no present. It therefore has no future. It belongs in the past, and to the past we should abandon it.

---

[15] Nostalgia has at least two expressions on the current scene. The critical and intellectual nostalgia that I am discussing here looks for solutions in dated theories or tries to recover an era in the past. In the last work of Michel Foucault, for example, although he constantly denies it, there is a tendency to represent the ascetic attitudes of ancient Greece as programmatic for modern ethics. A second sense of nostalgia has to do with the reading of literature, of giving it the respect of thinking with it, and of allowing conversants to feel not stupid but intelligent and "at home in the world." I see this as a continuation of techniques associated by the antiwar and women's movements with "consciousness raising" brought to the reading of literature in the classroom.

I do not want to mark a historical and political limit to these techniques. Both the antiwar and women's movements were organized according to the techniques and values invented by the civil rights movement, which confronted the skeptical politics of segregation with the ideals of integration, but these essentially white, middle-class movements quietly forgot their debt and responsibility to black intellectuals as they turned these same values against the divisive aims of the cold war era. Consequently, the black inventors of the dream of integration were excluded from its promise, the civil rights movement died, and Lyndon Johnson's war on poverty and racism was abandoned with the election of the conservative, Republican presidents of the seventies and eighties.

Index